Co-authoring in the Classroom

Co-authoring in the Classroom

Creating an Environment for Effective Collaboration

Helen Dale
University of Wisconsin–Eau Claire

National Council of Teachers of English
1111 W. Kenyon Road, Urbana, Illinois 61801-1096

Prepress: David Hamburg, Robert Heister, and Susan Huelsing
Humanities & Sciences Associates

Production Editor: Kurt Austin

Cover Art and Interior Design: Doug Burnett

Original TRIP Cover Design: Michael J. Getz

NCTE Stock Number: 06951-3050

Library of Congress Cataloging-in-Publication Data

Dale, Helen
    Co-authoring in the classroom: creating an environment for effective collaboration /Helen Dale.
            p. cm.
    Includes bibliographical references.
    ISBN 0-8141-0695-1
        1. English language—Composition and exercises—Study and teaching. 2. English language—Rhetoric—Study and teaching. 3. Authorship—Collaboration—Study and teaching. I. Title.
    PE1404.D355 1997
    808'.042'071—dc21   96-44498
                                                                                              CIP

Contents

Introduction

Currently, there has been an increased interest in collaborative writing because much of what we value in the teaching of writing supports writing *together*. The widely used process approach to teaching writing encourages student interaction. And cooperative learning, with its underlying social view of learning, leads naturally to valuing multiple voices. However, not many writing instructors encourage face-to-face collaborative writing or *co-authoring* as a means of engaging students with each other's ideas and writing processes. Unfortunately, when teachers think of collaborative writing or co-authoring, they often focus first on their reservations about it. They may not really know what constitutes effective co-authoring groups, or they do not know how to make those groups work smoothly. They may worry instead about issues such as individual accountability and evaluating a joint product.

Despite concerns such as these, teachers whose students write should not dismiss collaborative writing without at least attempting co-authoring groups. These groups are worth pursuing because students can potentially gain so much from the experience. At the heart of this monograph is the claim that collaborative writing is an effective tool for teaching writing. Through working with each other as co-authors, students learn important lessons about the processes and mechanics of writing, as well as lessons about working with others. Everything we know about the processes involved in collaborative writing leads us to see its great potential. But unless teachers give co-authoring a chance in real classroom environments, its potential remains *just* potential.

The purpose of this monograph is to explain co-authoring as a strategy for teaching writing; it will provide theoretical and research background for collaborative writing, a rationale for its use, and specific and practical suggestions for implementing co-authoring groups in classrooms.

Finding My Way to Collaborative Writing

My interest in collaborative writing began in the early seventies. At the time, I was teaching English at a Chicago-area high school whose English department chair prided himself on the amount of writing the students did. When he told me that my students were to write one essay per week, I complied, eager to do a good job. Only years later did I find out that most teachers in the department simply ignored that "rule." But I forged ahead. In addition to expressive writing, all of my 125 students wrote one formal essay each week, which I graded. Because at that time I interpreted "grading" as finding every mechanical and logical error, I soon became overwhelmed by the paper load. To survive, I had students write an occasional paper together in collaborative writing groups of three, just to catch my breath. Instead of twenty-seven papers, there were nine. I had made my job easier, but the price I paid was a feeling of guilt. I was apparently still working on the premise that the harder I worked and the more I suffered, the more my students would learn.

In time I overcame my guilt because the students were so clearly learning about writing from each other when they collaborated on a paper. As I circulated among the groups, I heard students talking seriously about ideas, sharing stories and details that supported those ideas, and discussing how to best organize their material. I saw students watching other students' minds at work as they composed aloud with and for each other. The isolation was gone, as was the mystery. Students learned how to plan before writing because a group simply cannot just begin.

Students in co-authoring groups learned various aspects of language from each other. Eric learned about commas from Wendy, not from me, because she had the information when he needed it. Students with weak mechanical skills could offer their input verbally, which allowed them to focus on meaning rather than blocking themselves by worrying about surface errors. Someone else was transcribing. Students also discussed more sophisticated elements of language such as connotation and word choice. One group in a tenth-grade English class tried out synonyms for "frightened" until they settled on "scared" because they wanted to describe childlike fears.

There were other benefits as well. Students got to know others in the class whom they would never have known before, and the sense of community that developed made subsequent classes run much more smoothly. Rather than being the primary authority, I could become a facilitator. Collaborative writing seemed to ease writing anxiety by providing a safe environment. I even used the groups to review for exams. Students wrote questions, and together they planned and wrote sample essay answers. For many, it eased the tension of writing essay exams.

Behavior and responsibility improved on collaborative writing days. Students were not tolerant of others who did not participate or were not prepared. Peer pressure was on my side. Letitia almost threw Gary out the window for not bringing in his draft on the day it was due. I came to his rescue, but he got the message. Students also learned things that had little to do with writing but were valuable nonetheless, such as standing up for themselves. Gina and Tom had to find a way to tell Michelle, a very assertive student, that her ideas for a particular assignment just did not work.

When I began teaching at a university, I still used collaborative writing occasionally, not to ease the paper load, but to help freshman composition students get to know one another and to learn from each other. Sharing responsibility made college writing less intimidating for freshmen. The co-authoring groups functioned very much as they did at the high school level, although college freshmen have more fixed writing strategies, so more negotiation has to take place. The students in co-authoring groups often chose each other as peer editors for individual writing assignments because they trusted others in their group. Janine, for instance, always wanted Sue as an editor because "she knows how to help me write less choppy." Co-authors discussed organization, ideas, mechanics, word choice, even style, and by discussing all of that, they developed a language for talking about writing, a metalanguage. Co-authoring groups create writing communities.

In workshops about collaborative writing, I spoke to Writing Project teachers from all grade levels and many subject areas, to English teachers from across the country, to those in writing-across-the-curriculum workshops, and to university faculty. Their questions and insights about collaborative writing enriched my thinking about the co-authoring process. But when they asked me for books or articles about establishing collaborative writing groups, there was little I could recommend. No studies described collaborative writing interactions in middle or secondary settings. With the needs of these teachers in mind, I conducted research on collaborative writing—research on the social context of co-authoring groups and their writing processes. Both cognitive and social contexts are discussed in this monograph because without a comfortable yet challenging social context, the cognitive benefits of collaborative writing simply do not occur.

Defining Collaborative Writing

The term *collaborative writing* itself is problematic. While it appears frequently in articles about both theoretical and instructional aspects of composition, it has a variety of meanings. The term is used to refer to cooperative planning as well as to writing separate sections of a text or to writing an entire text together. I use the term interchangeably with *co-authoring*. In this monograph, collaborative writing implies meaningful interaction and shared decision making and responsibility between group members in the writing of a shared document (Morgan et al., 1987).

When Ede and Lunsford (1990) studied collaborative writing in the workplace, most of what they observed was "hierarchical" co-authoring, in which writers divided up the work. Those who co-authored "dialogically," on the other hand, did not establish set roles; instead, they valued finding shared goals and blending voices. The process was an essential part of the product. This blended, dialogic model of collaborative writing seems to hold the most promise for writing instruction (Fleming, 1988) because it makes thinking about writing external and explicit (Flower & Higgins, 1991; Higgins, Flower & Petraglia, 1992).

Rationale

Collaborative writing has the potential to help both students and their teachers toward the goal of improved student writing. As children, we learn oral language in natural interactions by testing our own language hypotheses. Providing natural feedback for writing hypotheses should also presumably work well (Sperling, 1993), and collaborative writing provides a natural context for feedback about writing. In fact, students in co-authoring groups have been found to gain more from their interactions than students involved in peer editing (DiPardo & Freedman, 1988). Peer editing sessions "usually lack the intensity and focus that students experience when they share the work, responsibility, and grade" (Tobin, 1991, p. 65). There are many possible reasons for this.

When students write alone, they often have a difficult time generating ideas and sustaining a topic; this may be because writing does not provide them with a turn-taking partner, as does conversation. Collaborative writing also provides the oral prompts of conversation to help students bridge oral and written language. By its very nature a social activity, co-authoring can make the concept of audience real to students, often for the first time, because feedback on what they contribute orally is immediate. Co-authoring also has a real impact on the writing process. Writing together allows groups to examine the rhetorical situation and examine language choices (Rogers & Horton, 1992) and promotes a more recursive, more sophisticated writing process than that of students writing alone; it is a process more like that of expert writers (Dale, 1994a).

A real strength of collaborative writing is that by composing together, students observe others' minds at work, as co-authors reveal their thinking strategies and model their writing processes. This opening out of writing processes allows students to learn from each other in a natural way. It is also possible that children can better learn some aspects of writing from each other than from a teacher. Peers may be more effective than teachers at transforming knowledge about writing into usable skills, in part because their language and their perspectives may very well be similar (Daiute & Dalton, 1993). Because students reveal their thinking about writing when they co-author, we as teachers also gain in our knowledge of individual students' writing strategies. It allows us to "hear" students' thoughts about writing-in-process and to assess their contextualized needs. We may realize that the majority of the class misunderstands a basic concept, or we may find the key to helping a particular student with a recurrent writing problem.

Co-authoring places writing in the social and situated context of its use. That is helpful for students who are not always successful in the individualistic and competitive atmosphere of schools, because it provides an alternative and more social way of learning to write. Because students writing together are speaking, listening, writing, and reading, co-authoring is especially helpful to students whose first language is not English (Heap, 1989). Collaboration in writing may also be well suited to students from cultures that value a person's contribution to the group over individual achievement (Bosley, 1993). A by-product of such cross-cultural interactions is increased sensitivity and understanding of others (Sharan, 1980).

An important benefit of involving students in collaborative writing is that it helps to prepare them for writing in the workplace. Although professional writers, as well as those who work in government, business, and the professions, often collaborate (Ede & Lunsford, 1990), schools typically have given students neither formal instruction in co-authoring nor experience with writing together. This is unfortunate because the skills learned in group writing are needed in most businesses (Forman and Katsky, 1986). It is through co-authoring that students refine group skills and are exposed to various writing skills and processes.

By now it should be obvious that I am a real believer in co-authoring groups. Although I conducted research with as objective an eye as possible, my purpose here is different. I will try to avoid missionary zeal, but I believe strongly in the process of co-authoring as an important, but vastly underutilized, means of teaching students to write well. My goal is to explain some theoretical bases for collaborative writing, to clarify the co-authoring process, and to provide practical suggestions for establishing and maintaining collaborative writing groups. I hope that this monograph will encourage teachers of writing to try co-authoring groups in their classrooms.

1 Theory and Research

The two theoretical traditions that inform collaborative writing—social constructionism and cognition—offer strong support for its use in classrooms. Although these theoretical positions are sometimes viewed as opposed to one another, both offer important insights into knowledge construction. Theory and research in both communities point to thought processes as actually originating in social interaction (Palincsar, Stevens, and Gavelek, 1989; Vygotsky, 1978). Students benefit by internalizing each other's cognitive processes, arrived at by communicating socially (Damon, 1984). Neither view, by itself, provides an adequate picture of the writing act (Rubin, 1988).

SOCIAL THEORIES OF LANGUAGE

While the primary view of learning in the Western world has been Cartesian, a view which promotes the value of knowledge handed down by an authority, there has also been a minority view over the years, an argument for the social construction of learning. John Dewey (1938/1974) argued for the education of each individual in a community of learners. His constructionist approach to learning gained support from the work of George Herbert Mead, who believed meaning was constructed through social interaction. More recently, Brazilian Paolo Freire (1970) argued that literacy is best taught in social contexts; he envisioned effective education as "cointentional," with students actively involved in creating knowledge.

The study of collaborative writing is grounded in social constructionist theory. Those who see education and language through this lens credit the discourse community of any learning situation as the real source of knowledge and see writing as the manifestation of internalized social interactions. Kenneth Bruffee, who is often associated with this view, believes that to learn in a particular discourse community, one needs to talk with others in the community. In a writing classroom, then, talk about writing must occur because learning occurs socially. Viewed that way, writing is always collaborative at some level (Bruffee, 1984). Collaborative writing rests on social constructionist assumptions such as these.

Some of the most important contributions to the theoretical frameworks of social constructionism were made in the 1920s and 1930s by two Russians: Lev Vygotsky in developmental psychology and Mikhail Bakhtin in language/text study. However, their work did not become available in translation to the English-speaking world until relatively recently. Each is considered to be an influential language theorist, and each informs our concepts of learning and language production. Both envision thought, speech, and writing as dialogues with voices we already know through social contexts. The more voices we know, and the more interactions we have, the richer our language choices can be.

Vygotsky's Learning and Language Theories

Vygotsky's theoretical contributions (1978, 1981, 1986) help to explain the potential of co-authoring. His theories have many important implications for the epistemology of learning, but the simplest and most compelling is that by its very nature, learning is a social activity and is thus enhanced through social interactions. Through their social contacts, children learn new ideas and processes that stimulate their development. Later, these are internalized as abstract thought and "become part of the child's independent developmental achievement" (1978, p. 90).

It is the movement from interpersonal to intrapersonal that is not only at the heart of how we learn, but is also the link between Vygotsky's theories and the usefulness of co-authoring for writing instruction. In learning most processes, we can observe and internalize what we are capable of absorbing, but in writing that is not so. Usually very private, writing is not available for observation and imitation. Even in peer-response groups, all that is available for evaluation or learning is the product. Collaborative writing, on the other hand, makes people's thinking about writing external and explicit.

Another of Vygotsky's theoretical contributions was to redefine the relationship between development and learning (1978). In an important break from previous conceptions, he saw learning as leading, not following, development. That concept has important implications for education. The goal is to target teaching to the skills just beyond what a student is currently capable of achieving alone, what Vygotsky calls the "zone of proximal development." This is an area in which a child can accomplish—with adult guidance or the help of a more capable peer—what that child could not accomplish alone. Which student functions as the most capable peer in collaborative writing groups is flexible since there are so many points on which to *be* expert. The student who does not write well by most standards can suggest good ideas on which to build or can provide vigorous examples. In turn, that student has the opportunity to learn from another who organizes well, or keeps purpose and audience in mind, or delights in choosing a word for effect.

Although one teacher would have a hard time teaching within each student's zone of proximal development, collaborative writing groups can help achieve this end. First and quite simply, small groups reduce the number to be dealt with. Beyond that, co-authoring should allow students to maximize learning time in their zones. There is a good chance one peer is just slightly ahead of another on some aspect of thinking about writing or about the structure or mechanics of writing itself. No one can guarantee that any one co-authoring group or session will target effectively each student's learning zone, but there is a better chance of that happening in co-authoring groups than in large-group instruction.

In *Thought and Language* (1931/1986), Vygotsky addressed directly the most daunting problem of writing: the fact that it is a double abstraction—an abstraction from the sound of words and an abstraction from audience. It takes more words to express an idea in writing than in thought because the syntax of inner speech is abbreviated. To accommodate the absent audience, which needs more elaboration than inner speech provides, the writer must be conscious and deliberate.

Toward that end, collaborative writing can function as a bridge from inarticulate inner speech to socialized speech to writing, the most elaborated form of language. Because a collaborative writing group is trying to frame ideas in text and because it comprises at the same time writers and audience, the group can serve as intermediary. Speaking aloud a text-in-process demands the full elaboration that thinking can bypass and helps students to be precise and specific. The experience of being both writer and reader in a co-authoring group further helps students to be conscious of the audience's needs, an awareness that can be internalized.

Peer-group talk about writing takes advantage of the Vygotskian premise that speaking and writing are fundamentally social acts. Collaborative writing encourages voices to be heard, allows the prompts of oral conversation, and provides internalization of content and strategies from a social context.

Bakhtin and Dialogism

Like Vygotsky, Bakhtin (1981) emphasizes the socially constructed nature of language. What Bakhtin adds is an emphasis on struggle and voice. He contextualizes the study of language use and development by inviting us to see language as fully interactional, as arising from our various cultural contexts. Bakhtin's work supports co-authoring because it provides a rationale for interaction during the writing process and offers a social explanation of the value of conflict toward language growth. His theory of dialogism is a way of understanding language as part of a larger whole where all the possible meanings of a word interact, possibly conflict, and affect future meanings.

It is all too easy, but misleading, to conceive of dialogism as dialogue. Rather, dialogism refers to the context in which an utterance exists and the relationship of one utterance to another, not to the number of speakers (Phelps, 1989). Even our thoughts are dialogic because they come from all of our associations; they arise out of what Bakhtin calls *heteroglossia*, the incorporation of *"another's speech in another's language"* (1981, p. 324, emphasis in original).

According to Bakhtin, no one ever writes alone, because writing is the result of our interactions with the world. What each of us speaks or writes expresses not just individual values and beliefs, but also those of the cultural context. Since our thoughts and words are dialogized, socializing the writing context simply contributes to a richer language environment. Co-authoring brings voice to thought that is dialogic to begin with.

Collaborative writing externalizes the divergent voices of text-in-process. This can help to create the productive cognitive conflict that leads to growth in language. Because competing words, ideas, and styles are expressed out loud, students are better able to learn from them. Writing together engages students in a process that enriches language; through verbal interaction we learn language options.

When students write together, they affirm what they know about writing and can learn from each other by engaging in what Bakhtin calls "internally persuasive discourse" (1981, p. 345): shared language that has the capacity to "interanimate relationships with new contexts" (p. 346). Through such discourse, students co-construct their knowledge of writing. This social form of learning can be much more effective for some learners than the "authoritative discourse" (p. 343) of traditional writing instruction.

All this talk about multiple voices and collaboration makes some educators exceedingly nervous about individual accomplishment and the concept of ownership in writing. In the end, we often do have to produce writing alone, it is true, but collaborative writing groups, rather than working against the goals of writing instruction, can provide instead a learning situation. Dialogism never denies that our thoughts can be our own; rather, it explains our thoughts as originally conceived in a social context that was internalized. We can write individually, but only by having already joined a conversation of voices. We can develop an individual style, but only by being exposed to many other styles. The more voices we hear, then the more choices we have, and the more fluent is our own. Through shared language, we create ourselves.

Bakhtin compares learning from others with a chemical union; a chemical bond creates something new, yet the original elements are still there as part of the new substance. Collaborative writing fits this metaphor. The voice of each student is there, but as a new substance, reflecting the exchange of ideas and voices. Co-authoring groups are exceptionally well designed to prompt active language learning and to allow for the verbal exchanges that Bakhtin would see as the base of learning itself and its expression through writing.

RESEARCH ON LANGUAGE AND LEARNING

Cooperative Learning

Collaborative writing is strongly supported by a substantial research base in cooperative learning, which can be defined as "students working together in a group small enough that everyone can participate on a collective task . . . without the direct and immediate supervision of the teacher" (Cohen, 1994, p. 3). In these groups, "students work together to maximize their own and each other's learning" (Johnson & Johnson, 1994, p. 61). During the past two decades, research has "established beyond a doubt that children can have a powerful influence upon one another's intellectual development" (Damon, 1984, p. 331). Over the years, literally hundreds of studies have been done on cooperative learning. A review of that body of research in education concludes that cooperative learning benefits students of all ages, in all subject areas, and in a wide variety of tasks (Bossert, 1988). Working together toward a shared goal leads to higher achievement than working alone, and it leads to gains in the kinds of thinking teachers like to model for students: high-level reasoning, generation of new ideas, and transfer of knowledge from one situation to another (Johnson & Johnson, 1994).

The benefits seem to be affective as well as cognitive. The affective aspects of cooperative learning are both positive and significant. Having peers with whom to solve school tasks contributes to higher self-esteem, more positive attitudes toward school, more positive relationships with all peers, and the ability to view situations from another's perspective (Johnson & Johnson, 1985; Sharan, 1980). Not only can cooperative learning contribute to a positive classroom climate, but it is also linked to learning, which is increased when students are allowed to use each other as resources (Cohen, Lotan, & Leechor, 1989; Johnson & Johnson, 1994). Through interdependence, students feel less uncertain about the task, which is particularly helpful for those who need assistance. That is not to say that cooperative learning benefits only the weaker students. It also promotes higher-order thinking. In negotiating a representation of the task, students in groups think more abstractly than do individual students. That is a benefit to confident students, and exposure to high-level reasoning allows weaker students to learn from stronger ones (Cohen, 1994).

Working together on a project can involve authentic learning for students. Peer groups concentrate on what the student learns, not on what the teacher knows. In groups, students need to *do* something: communicate, organize, interpret, or apply. In traditional teaching practice, all this is done by the teacher: "The teacher's activity makes the traditional method a very effective method of learning—for the teacher" (Bouton & Garth, 1983, p. 78). What we teach is what we really come to learn; we should promote that active learning for our students.

One of the biggest objections to cooperative learning in general and collaborative writing in particular is that the academically more successful student will be taken advantage of. However, "the research provides absolutely no support for this claim; high achievers gain from cooperative learning" (Slavin, 1989, p. 237). There are several reasons why this is so. In working on the goals of the assignment, students must explicate their strategies, which serves a metacognitive function. By giving procedural help, students progress (Mugny & Doise, 1978; Peterson et al., 1984). Research on peer writing tutors, for instance, finds consistently that the tutors not only increase their knowledge of written language, but also acquire new strategies for understanding writing tasks (Matsuhashi et al., 1989). Another factor is the cognitive growth that verbalizing promotes (Brown & Palincsar, 1989; Deering & Meloth, 1990). When you have to teach ideas or strategies to others, you learn them well.

Verbalization

That verbalizing is the biggest factor behind the success of cooperative learning in all its forms has been generally agreed upon by researchers during the past thirty years (Bargh & Schul, 1980; Brown & Palincsar, 1989;

Deering & Meloth, 1990; Gagne & Smith, 1962; Johnson & Johnson, 1985; Johnson et al., 1985; Perret-Clermont, 1980; Webb, 1982; Wittrock, 1974). Because it is social, learning occurs through conversation. Students who verbalize about what they're learning comprehend more fully than those who don't, and the more explaining a student does, the more benefits that student receives (Cohen 1994). That is why the highest-achieving students gain from the opportunity to verbalize their ideas. Even recall of information is affected by verbalization. When working in pairs, students who speak about information recall significantly more ideas than those assigned a listener's role (Spurlin et al., 1984).

Requiring verbalization forces students to think of reasons for the choices they make as they think through a problem or issue (Gagne & Smith, 1962). One particularly interesting finding in verbalization research is that students vocalizing to a peer performed better than those doing so for an experimenter. Purpose, then, must be an important factor. Students who were genuinely engaged in the process of teaching others learned more than those still cast in the role of student (Bargh & Schul, 1980; Durling & Schick, 1976). When we are in a position to explain material or strategies to others, we strengthen our own cognitive organization and learn more completely.

One real strength of collaborative writing is that when students co-author, they must talk about writing and about ideas. Verbalization is inherent in the process. The social context allows students to think out loud, which, in turn, provides an opportunity to think not only about the ideas involved, but also about writing itself (Daiute & Dalton, 1993; Dale, 1994b). The thoughts that writers never speak aloud, their internalized dialogue about writing, can be analyzed when those thoughts are externalized for co-authors (Dale, 1994b; Rogers & Horton, 1992). Not only can other students learn new writing strategies by listening to their peers, but students can find solutions they did not even know they had by listening to themselves.

The connection between talk and writing cannot be overemphasized, yet writing instructors do not take advantage of that connection often enough. When teachers ask students to collaborate by serving as peer editors for almost-finished drafts, they often provide worksheets or edit sheets for student writers. In that context, students can quietly read each other's papers and fill out worksheets and never even speak to each other about writing or the issues raised in the particular piece. When that happens, "students are bound by context to limited roles and responsibilities . . ." (Sperling, 1993, p. 14). It is important that students have the opportunity to talk to each other when they write because we learn by internalizing the talk around us (Vygotsky, 1931/1986). We learn more than facts through talk; we also hear thinking modeled. Therefore, if we talk about writing, we also learn to think about it.

Cognitive Conflict

Cognitive conflict occurs with the recognition that one's ideas are different from another person's or are incompatible with new information (Daiute & Dalton, 1988). This positive conflict is the mediator between students' verbal interactions and the way they reorganize cognitively to accommodate new concepts. Like the catalyst in a chemical reaction, it is not present in the final product but is nonetheless indispensable (Perret-Clermont, 1980). Students in groups restructure their thoughts by comparing new information to information previously acquired and modify or replace an existing concept or attitude if that seems necessary (Webb, 1982). Johnson and Johnson, who have worked for years with cooperative learning and the conflict it entails, believe that in a cooperative situation with a supportive climate where students feel comfortable enough to challenge each other's ideas, conflict is a positive force that too many teachers avoid or suppress. By doing so, teachers lose valuable opportunities to increase students' cognitive development (Johnson & Johnson, 1979). When students learn through positive cognitive conflict, the very means of acquiring new concepts is based on an active process of learning (Myers & Lamm, 1976).

Some cognitive conflict is an inevitable part of the process of collaborative writing because students must negotiate differences of opinion in order to arrive at consensus (Dale, 1994b). While co-authoring, students might, for instance, offer alternative suggestions about phrasing or organization. Those alternatives force them to justify their own choices and consider the reasoning of others in the group on some aspect of writing.

A number of studies find that cognitive conflict is a vital component of successful collaborative writing (Burnett, 1994a; Daiute & Dalton, 1988; Dale, 1994b). It only makes sense that a group which merely agrees to one member's suggested text is less involved in the writing process than a group which challenges its members to clarify reasoning and support ideas. Burnett's study (1994a) showed a strong correlation between the quality of written work and the amount of substantive engagement in the collaborative writing group. That correlation can be easily explained. When students consider alternatives, they examine the strengths and weaknesses of various points, allowing them to choose their strongest arguments. In a study of ninth-grade co-authors, Dale (1994b) found cognitive conflict to be one of the most important factors in separating a model group of writers from a typical or problem group. For the most successful group, 20 percent of all the co-authored discourse involved cognitive conflict. The more typical group spent 11 percent of all its talk engaged in cognitive conflict, and the least successful group, only 7 percent. The group that had the most trouble tended to let one person do the writing without offering alternatives. The ideas in the paper, therefore, went unchallenged.

Words like *conflict* and *challenge* are, perhaps, unfortunate since they sound almost combative. Co-authors need not be in conflict to write well together, but they must be engaged with each other and the writing project to the extent that they care to contribute their ideas and question those of others. They must be adequately in tune with the writing to hear awkward language and suggest alternative phrasing. If students are comfortable with each other in a supportive classroom environment, they can debate both ideas and phrasing without negative social consequences.

RESEARCH ON COGNITION AND WRITING/ COLLABORATIVE WRITING PROCESSES

Strategic Thinking

One claim of the literature on collaboration is that for knowledge which involves judgments, we learn best through communicating with, and even relying on, our peers. Since writing is a process involving multiple judgments—about what to write, how to start, how to say what you mean—learning writing collaboratively can be very effective (Bruffee, 1985). While this assumes that knowledge can be socially constructed, there is also a cognitive component. Co-authoring's potential is based to a large extent on the assumption that collaborative writing allows students to observe alternative cognitive processes and strategies unfolding on a shared topic (Daiute, 1986; Dale, 1992; O'Donnell et al., 1985). Through that shared process, they can learn new strategies themselves. By opening up their previously tacit writing processes, students can add to their repertoire of writing strategies, as well as become aware of their own.

Other areas of research that are helpful in understanding collaborative writing are research on the differences between novice and expert writers and research on the writing process. The first explanation of the composing process was advanced in 1965 with the Rohman/

Wlecke model (Bizzell, 1986). They found that effective writing could be classified into three linear stages: prewriting, writing, and editing—terms that are used almost universally now in writing classrooms. By the 1980s, research methodologies such as think-aloud protocols focused on the processes of writers (Emig, 1971; Faigley et al., 1985; Flower & Hayes, 1980, 1981a, 1981b; Perl, 1979; Sommers, 1980). The plural—*processes*—is important to note since writing processes are not the same for all people and vary with the kind of writing being done (Bizzell, 1986; Britton et al., 1975; Emig, 1971). The recursiveness observed in the writing process led to a very different conception of how writers compose. The most widely known model of the composing process is that of Flower and Hayes (1981a). It includes subprocesses such as generating ideas, organizing, and setting goals. Putting ideas down on paper so that they are visible creates a heavy mental load for inexperienced writers who must consider handwriting or keyboarding, mechanics, word choice, syntax, organization, and higher-level concerns such as clarity, purpose, and audience (Humes, 1983). Reviewing, a stage of the writing process that can occur at any time, leads to evaluation and includes revision. For experienced writers, much of this is automated, but for novice writers, the task can seem formidable.

Because collaborative writing prompts students to write more recursively, and in that sense more like accomplished writers (Dale, 1994a), research that compares the cognitive processes of expert and novice writers is important to the study of co-authoring. Research on the composing process also helps to explain the advantages of co-authoring because that literature suggests productive ways to compose, ways that collaborative writing promotes. While just explaining what we know about the recursive stages of the writing process may be helpful to students, collaborative writing allows students to experience others as they model the processes. Since co-authors are exposed to alternative strategies and ideas, they have an awareness of possibilities that they could not otherwise know.

Planning and Revising

Planning is an important stage that separates effective writers from ineffective ones (Flower & Hayes, 1981a). Experienced writers have a complex goal network in planning both content and process; they also keep the purpose of the writing and the needs of the audience in mind (Bereiter & Scardamalia, 1987; Flower & Hayes, 1981a, 1981b; Higgins, Flower, & Petraglia, 1992; Rubin, 1988). Novice writers, on the other hand, do not plan enough at any point in the writing process (Bereiter & Scardamalia, 1982; Bridwell, 1980; Emig, 1971; Flower & Hayes, 1981a; Flower et al., 1994; Perl, 1979; Pianko, 1979). Perl, for instance, found that her college writers spent only about an average of four minutes planning during the prewriting phase. Pianko observed college writers spending only 1.26 minutes to makes decisions before they began to write. None had complete conceptions of where the essay was going before they began. If college writers plan this little, we can assume that most younger writers plan even less than this research reports.

Collaborative writing encourages planning. When writing together, students cannot just begin; they must plan and organize. In a study of ninth graders co-authoring, Dale (1994b) found that 14 percent of all co-authoring discourse was spent representing the writing task, and another 25 percent on strategic talk about planning. As writing instructors know from experiences with student writers, for students to spend more than a quarter of their time planning is rare indeed. As a measure of comparison, Durst's 1987 study of eleventh-grade writers found that only 13 percent of the conversational turns related to *any* aspect of the writing process. When students write alone, they tend to worry about whether they have enough to say rather than "doing the energetic, constructive planning" (Wallace, 1994b, p. 48) that experienced writers engage in.

Collaborative writing also helps novice writers with revision. For experienced writers, the whole composing process is one of revision because their writing processes are so recursive (Bridwell, 1980; Flower & Hayes, 1981a; Sommers, 1980). As they write, they trigger new ideas and evaluate them. However, when novice writers revise, they make only surface changes (Sommers, 1980), often prematurely, thus stopping the flow of their ideas (Perl, 1979). Collaborative writing alters the way the composing process is organized (Heap, 1989). For co-authors, planning and revising are all but inseparable and are done throughout the writing process (Dale, 1994a), much in the way more experienced writers proceed.

Novice writers composing alone tend to produce "writer-based" prose (Flower, 1979). Since they know what they mean, they cannot imagine that anyone else does not know, so they do not provide the audience with all the information needed. But co-authors get built-in feedback from their peers. There is an automatic focus on audience. Suggestions for content, organization, and word choice are often negotiated, taking into account the reactions of an immediate audience: the other co-authors. When students write individually, they may or may not have internalized, conversational partners (Bereiter & Scardamalia, 1987) and so may not question their processes, but students co-authoring must verbalize their inner questions to get the help of the group. In peer-response groups, students who ask for help often do not receive it (Freedman, 1987, 1992), but in a co-authoring context, students have every incentive to focus on process as they help each other. Talking through a paper gives students a look at the big picture, rather than focusing on individual mechanical concerns; it provides a window on others' writing strategies.

RESEARCH ON CO-AUTHORING

Despite its potential, there is a surprisingly small amount of published research on collaborative writing. There are a number of recent studies that use the term *collaborative writing,* but most often they refer to students helping each other in the planning phase of individual papers (Flower & Higgins, 1991; Higgins, Flower, & Petraglia, 1992; Flower et al., 1994) rather than co-authoring. Ede and Lunsford have written about collaborative writing and posit that only by *writing* together—not just brainstorming or editing—can students really learn from one another (Ede & Lunsford, 1983, 1985). Their primary contribution has been to study collaborative writing in the professions, where they found that the vast majority of professionals write together some of the time (1985, 1990), a finding that corroborates the work of Faigley and Miller (1982). A number of studies exist in the fields of business and technical communication which show that it is common practice for employees to write together. Rogers and Horton (1992) studied groups of employees at an electronic data systems office who were co-authoring. The authors found that what they call "face-to-face" collaboration gave co-authors a real advantage over writing individually. Co-authoring helped writers better understand their task, appraise their decisions more fully, examine their language choices, and consider ethics in their decisions.

A few studies examine college writers co-authoring. Rebecca Burnett (1992, 1994a) focuses on collaborative planning in her research and finds that college writers who work with a peer tend to avoid expressing differences of opinion. Since cognitive conflict is a positive influence in writing, her goal was to prompt writers to "make visible" their thinking and their differences of opinion. Another study (O'Donnell et al., 1985) focuses on the written product and suggests that students write with more clarity and detail when co-authoring than when writing alone. A recent study of co-authors in first-year composition found that their written products were far better than those written by individual writers the previous semester (Hillebrand, 1994).

Many of the published studies on collaborative writing take place in elementary school settings. Hilgers (1987) suggests that young children be taught cooperation skills before co-authoring so that they will not spend their energies trying to control the group and the text. Three articles that examine the actual discourse of students writing together find that students have much to gain from their interactions. Daiute (1986) found collaborative writing to be a subtle form of learning in which students share their ideas about good writing and their composing strategies. A later study (Daiute & Dalton, 1988) found that co-authoring produces the social-cognitive dissonance that can lead to effective learning about writing, an experience with questioning one's own point of view, and better written products. Daiute and Dalton (1993) have more recently found that young co-authors help each other in many different ways while they write. Since each student contributes to the effort from his or her own writing expertise, over time students learn the most if they write with partners who have expertise which is different from their own. Another advantage they see is that collaboration "encourages children to express and reflect on thinking that might otherwise remain unexamined or unelaborated" (p. 293).

The only study I am aware of that investigates the co-authoring processes of middle school or secondary students is the one I conducted (Dale 1992). That research finds the success of co-authoring affected by the students' level of engagement, the level of cognitive conflict, and the predominance of positive social interactions. Much more research needs to be done to understand what takes place between collaborators of different kinds and in different contexts. With that understanding, we may find collaborative writing to be not only an effective way of learning to write, but also an excellent means of preparing students for writing in the professions.

SUMMARY

The concept of writing collaboratively is founded on some basic assumptions about writers, writing, and learning. The theoretical bases of co-authoring help us to understand its benefits to writers. This chapter emphasized the background and potential of co-authoring and covered the following points:

- Writing is a social process. We learn—and learn to write—from the outside in.

- Talk in a community of writers is an important source of learning for writers.
- Co-authoring externalizes thinking about writing and makes it explicit.
- Co-authoring focuses student attention on audience by making students simultaneously writers and readers.
- Co-authoring allows students to incorporate into their own repertoires concepts, strategies, and language patterns of their peers.
- Co-authoring focuses on higher-order thinking: generating new ideas, reasoning, and transferring knowledge from one situation to another.
- Co-authoring promotes positive attitudes toward self, others, and school.
- Co-authoring encourages positive cognitive conflict.
- Co-authoring prompts students to write more recursively, in a process more like that of expert writers.
- Co-authoring emphasizes planning.

2 Practice

PREPARING TO WRITE TOGETHER

Despite years of research claiming the virtues of cooperative learning, despite the fact that many teachers use small-group work as a regular part of their classes, despite the fact that the process approach to teaching writing encourages the use of peer writing groups, whenever I plan to observe an English class, I often hear, "That's not really a good time to come. The students are just meeting in writing groups." Behind that statement lie misguided assumptions about the teaching and learning of English: that facilitating writing groups is not teaching and that students do not learn unless knowledge, which is a fixed entity, is being transmitted from the authority—the teacher—to students—the receivers (Gere, 1990; Onore, 1989).

Another assumption exists in most schools: that competition is the norm and that students learn best by competing. But this assumption, too, needs to be reconsidered; few students learn best by competing with others. The positive learning outcomes associated with competition are based on what Alfie Kohn (1986) refers to as a series of myths. When schools foster competition, they often fail to recognize the importance of collaboration. Mary Belenky, one of the authors of *Women's Ways of Knowing* (1986), sees collaboration as vital to education and the current competitive model for learning as "irrational" (Ashton-Jones & Thomas, 1990).

While I do not think that all competition is counterproductive, I do puzzle over why there is so much resistance to collaboration as though *it* were irrational. Part of the answer certainly lies in the issue of authority. From the time preservice teachers are "trained," control is presented as a major issue. When teachers institute groups of any kind, they relinquish some control. Noise levels go up, and students who are engaged look happy and animated. Since we have all been taught to be suspicious of such behavior, we wonder if students can learn while they are having fun. Further, if groups are functioning well, they don't need you at that moment, and a teacher may wonder what to do with him- or herself. Perhaps this is why only 63 percent of the fifty-four ninth-grade English classes involved in a recent study included any small-group work at all. More surprising is that in those classes that did incorporate group work, small-group activity lasted, on average, only about two minutes a day (Nystrand & Gamoran, 1996).

Another reason teachers sometimes resist groups and all forms of collaborative writing is their concern that students and parents oppose collaboration, afraid that the student will be taken advantage of in some way. The premise seems to be that if a bright child or one with particular knowledge shares her expertise, then somehow her intelligence and potential for success are diminished. Everything we know about the benefits of verbalizing our knowledge refutes that position. Until teachers can give students and their parents sound explanations of why collaboration is beneficial, learning communities will continue to resist collaboration. One of the aims of this monograph, in fact, is to give teachers sensible answers for objections to collaboration.

Competition is so much a part of our culture that—like fish in water—we fail to recognize its existence. To write in a competitive setting simply does not make sense academically, socially, or professionally. If our aim as teachers is to prepare students to express themselves, interact, and communicate in various settings, then including experience with collaborative writing is essential. At present there is a real dichotomy between the way writing is taught and the way it is practiced in the "real world." In the workplace, people often write together, but writing is so rarely taught as a collaborative practice that we do not even have a vocabulary to describe what happens when people write together (Ede & Lunsford, 1986). Offering students the opportunity to work together allows them to develop collaborative skills that do not always come naturally to them. By engaging students in collaborative writing, we serve two important goals: (1) to improve the individual student's writing through a heightened awareness of audience perception and (2) to prepare all students for successful collaboration in both personal and work contexts.

PREPARING YOURSELF/THE TEACHER'S ROLE

Authority in the Classroom

A cynical response to co-authoring is that it is "the blind leading the blind." But that cliché assumes that knowledge is an entity given by an authority. It is no accident that "author" and "authority" have the same root word (Onore, 1989). To be an effective author, you need to feel some authority about your subject and about composing. When knowledge about writing is created by a community of peers, students can teach each other to write "in new and potentially significant ways"

(Trimbur, 1985, p. 88). Collaborative writing groups are a good vehicle for that learning.

When teachers engage students in co-authoring, they encourage writers to negotiate meaning and to learn literacy strategies from each other. The teacher becomes a facilitator of learning rather than a transmitter of knowledge. That distinction requires an adjustment for some teachers because the shift in authoring entails a shift in authority. It is difficult for some teachers to accept that learning can go on without direct instruction. The issue of control is an important one. "Controlling" groups does not necessarily mean direct supervision. By delegating authority, teachers are not giving up control. Rather, they are controlling the classroom environment in other ways (Cohen, Lotan, & Leechor, 1989). It is important to give students as much control as possible over their learning and to be aware of actions that can affect authority. For instance, when a teacher "arrives" to stand near or sit in on a group, students often stop directing their own talk (Cohen, 1994). The more autonomy students have, the more knowledge they will produce themselves, and the more likely it is that collaborative work will contribute positively to their learning (Nystrand, Gamoran, & Heck, 1992).

Re-envisioning the Writing Classroom

When we as teachers incorporate collaborative writing into the classroom repertoire, we have to re-envision some aspects of teaching writing because we are in "new intellectual territory. Our cultural traditions don't prepare us very well for collaborative ways of teaching and learning . . ." (Spear, 1993). Writing classrooms which use collaborative writing are based on the premise that writing is a social act. Such classrooms look and sound different from traditional English classrooms. Students do not do less work; they do different work. While traditional writing classes value as learning a "safe arrival," classes in which students co-author value learning that occurs during the "vicissitudes of the trip" (Sperling, 1993, p. 7).

In such classrooms, teachers have redefined their role. The goal is "to help students gain authority over their knowledge and gain independence in using it" (Bruffee, 1985, p. 49). Not everyone, however, agrees about how best to do that. Some believe that collaborative writing works best when students are left alone because a teacher joining a group can undermine the development of student authority (Weiner, 1986) or "unintentionally undermine the source of learning, that is, the interaction of students" (Cohen, Lotan, & Leechor, 1989, p. 92). Lad

Tobin wants "students to learn to argue, negotiate, and compromise as writers," so he "stay[s] out of the initial planning as much as possible" (1991, p. 65). Others disagree and believe that when facilitating groups, teachers must intervene in order to "save" the group without getting involved (Goldstein & Malone, 1985). Some believe in a modified stance, for instance, that a teacher's expertise may be required only when young children engaged in a specific task have exhausted their potential for meaningful exchange (Daiute & Dalton, 1993). Despite these seeming differences, it is important to recognize that all those who advocate collaborative writing make two assumptions: (1) that students have been well prepared to collaborate on a specific writing task and (2) that the writing task is designed to benefit from collaboration.

One way to prepare for collaborative writing, then, is to decide how comfortable you are with your students not always needing you; that will determine, in part, to what extent you will sit in on groups. My own feeling is that if students are well prepared for the assignment, are given an assignment for which collaboration makes sense, and understand the most productive ways to co-author, then the best way for a teacher to use her time is to observe students. In circulating and listening to groups writing together, you can gain real insights into students' writing processes as well as their strengths and weaknesses. I have learned at least as much about my students from close observation while they co-authored as from evaluating their papers—probably more.

Another aspect of writing together that is important to understand is the recursiveness of the co-authoring process. Students do not brainstorm day one, write day two, and revise day three. Co-authoring blends the "stages" of the writing process to such an extent that it becomes hard to distinguish planning from revising. When students are speaking text together, you can literally hear the recursiveness of the writing process. One student might start a sentence, another finish it, and a third suggest a new word or give advice on mechanics. It is important to know that co-authoring takes more class time than writing individually because of its emphasis on negotiation. Another important point is that collaborative writing places evaluation and "covering" the curriculum in a secondary position to the *learning* of writing.

Understanding Group Functioning

To be of the most assistance to students who will be writing together, teachers should have some knowledge about groups and understand why some behaviors and attitudes help the group to function well and why some are ineffective. Because "the behavior called for in a cooperative small group is radically different from the behavior called for in a conventional classroom setting" (Cohen, 1994, p. 26), we need to provide guidelines for successful interactions. If we put students in groups and say no more, we cannot expect all students to have positive experiences. We cannot assume that students will blindly follow rules we establish, nor can we assume that students' common sense will carry them through; "neither prescription nor intuition is likely to work . . ." (Warburton, 1987, p. 305).

One place to look for guidance is the business world, where teamwork is essential to the success of an organization. Business analysts have identified characteristics of effective teams (Parker, 1990), and many of those characteristics apply to collaborative writing groups. Writing groups should know the following about teams that function well:

- They have a purpose and a general plan.
- They communicate effectively—i.e., they listen to each other and allow everyone to participate.
- They arrive at decisions by taking into account all views, and when they disagree, they do so in a pleasant way.
- They share leadership and value the diverse abilities of the group members.
- They self-assess.

The last point needs to be emphasized. Groups must become aware of their interpersonal and writing processes and learn to talk about how their members are doing as a group. Making students aware of those metacognitive patterns takes some time, but it is time well spent because process knowledge makes groups more effective.

Assigning Roles in Groups

While some teachers believe that assigning roles for group work helps students to become more accountable, I find roles in co-authoring groups to do more harm than good. A common perception is that students in structured groups with assigned roles necessarily learn more than when the structure is more open. That is far from true. In a study of learning in groups, researchers found that students in groups without assigned roles did better than students who had their roles assigned to them (Ross & Raphael, 1990). There are subtle issues to consider as well as those measured by standardized tests. When roles are assigned in groups, those roles often differ in status (Miller & Harrington, 1990), so some students have more responsibility than others. To understand how students divide responsibility, a teacher can circulate and observe whether students distribute authority and roles, and if they do, how they do so. If one of the goals of establishing collaborative writing groups in a classroom is to distribute authority in the classroom, then assigning roles undercuts that initiative.

Even if the focus is on the quality of writing, rather than on how students organize themselves, assigning roles still seems counterproductive because in a co-authoring context, writers tend to concentrate more on satisfying the role than on participating in text production. What contributes much more to learning is for students to become aware of themselves as writers, to understand the ways they interact in writing groups, and for teachers to be aware of how their students function when co-authoring. If a teacher is concerned about students' abilities to write together, solutions other than assigning roles might work better. Depending on the class and the amount of cooperative learning the students had experienced previously, the students might benefit from some team-building activities. It very well might suffice to have students write some short pieces together first and focus on their interactions before they co-author a longer piece.

Later in this chapter, collaborative writing exercises will be presented, along with a discussion of factors that affect the success of a group. Knowing your students' interaction patterns and the factors that most affect good co-authoring could be critical in facilitating functional groups. Students must recognize the uniqueness of each member's perspective. That attitude will allow students to feel comfortable about making differences explicit so that the group can resolve those differences. If students know that resolving conflict is critical, they are more likely to be actively engaged than they would be had they merely been assigned a role. At a more general level, students must understand the principles of group work and of active listening and must learn to be sensitive to the demands of the context (Warburton, 1987).

PREPARING STUDENTS

Understanding the Rationale/Asking Questions

Before beginning collaborative writing with a class, it is important to give students a rationale for its use. The benefit students most readily understand is that collaborative problem solving and co-authoring are practices used frequently by those who work in government, business, and industry. Surveys of those in the professions reveal that between 75 to 87 percent of respondents sometimes collaborate in writing (Ede & Lunsford, 1990; Faigley & Miller, 1982). Despite this evidence, most current models of teaching writing focus solely on single authorship. Students who have had no preparation in co-authoring will be unprepared for some writing tasks in the workplace. That is not to say that co-authoring in the classroom is exactly the same as that done in the workforce (Burnett, 1994b). For instance, while face-to-face collaboration on writing tasks is frequent in business, collaborative drafting is not. That may be because writers do not have enough past experience to do it well (Rogers & Horton, 1992). But despite the differences between school and work co-authoring, the attitudes toward collaboration, the ability to recognize productive interactions, and the habits of mind that it instills cannot but help students who have such school experiences perform more comfortably as co-authors in the workplace than those who have not. Our job as teachers is to help students learn to deal with the frustrations as well as enjoy the positive aspects of co-authoring.

Other benefits are acquired as well. Through co-authoring, students learn to cooperate and negotiate, skills which are invaluable in other situations. They experience audience directly, and through the direct and immediate feedback, they learn to be more sensitive to a reader's needs. Co-authoring can also teach writers new strategies: the majority of students who have co-authored over the years in my classrooms have found that they learn new ways to brainstorm and plan.

Since collaborative writing alters students' roles and responsibilities in the classroom, they need to have an opportunity to ask questions and to express any anxieties they feel about co-authoring. Assume that they may have some genuine concerns. Students may want to know, for instance, the extent to which their grades might be affected by co-authored pieces. My students are reassured that their individual contribution will be taken into account as I determine their grade. The specifics about evaluation will be addressed in more detail later in this chapter. The point, for now, is that their concerns must be taken seriously.

Combating Misconceptions

Both students and their parents may well be suspicious of collaborative writing—schools have focused so heavily on competition that students may assume that anyone else's gain is their loss. But that simply is not true. "Good" writers worry that others may not do enough work or will not be adept enough as writers. Research discussed in the "Theory and

Research" section of this monograph points out that the student who talks the most, contributes the most, and writes the most also gains the most benefit. When students explain their own knowledge and strategies, they increase their knowledge of written language. An important factor is the teacher's attitude; teacher beliefs about learning to write affect how students approach writing (Freedman, 1987). If the teacher believes in the gains students can make by sharing their strategic knowledge about writing, the students and their families will learn to trust the process, too.

Explaining Multiple Intelligences/Abilities

For students to work together effectively in small groups of any kind, and that includes co-authoring groups, they need to be taught new classroom norms (Cohen, Lotan, & Leechor, 1989). Students need new ways to look at learning. They need to see their peers as *resources* rather than as competitors; one way to do that is to make students aware of their own talents and capacities and those of their peers. New learning principles such as the principle of multiple intelligences (Gardner, 1983; Smagorinsky, 1991) and the multiple-abilities treatment (Cohen, 1986; Tammivaara, 1982) are uncomplicated and offer positive ways to view the capacity for learning.

Gardner (1983) points out that schools have historically valued only a few of the ways in which people can be intelligent, rewarding in particular linguistic and logical/mathematical skills. But there are other intelligences that we would do well to respect in school: the musical, spatial, bodily/kinesthetic, interpersonal, and intrapersonal. By honoring more of these intelligences, we will allow more students to succeed in school and to feel good about the work they do. Peter Smagorinsky (1991) has taken Gardner's seven intelligences and adapted them for the English classroom.

When we ask students to write together, we are clearly honoring linguistic talent. Other kinds of intelligence are honored in collaborative writing, too. In focusing on organization, groups can use the talents of a student with logical/mathematical intelligence and certainly need members with interpersonal intelligence so that the discussion will run smoothly and all members will feel included. Another intelligence is the intrapersonal, and students with this talent are capable of understanding themselves and how they write and function in groups. This metacognitive strength can be useful when co-authors have to analyze how the group process affects both the writing process and the paper that results from the collaboration. Other kinds of intelligence—musical, kinesthetic, or spatial—do not work explicitly in collaborative writing unless the work to be done is more like a project. Then students can contribute by composing song lyrics, dancing, or making maps.

When applied to the classroom, the multiple-abilities treatment (Cohen, 1994) is similar to that of multiple intelligences; the basic premise is that schools should find ways for all students to participate in classroom activities. In order for all students to learn, they must be convinced that they all have abilities that contribute to group work. Cohen and Lotan (1995) discuss two classroom interventions to achieve that end: (1) multiple abilities and (2) assigning competencies.

In the multiple-abilities treatment, Cohen wants teachers and their students to understand that the complex tasks that groups work on involve many kinds of skills and abilities. For the work to be done, no one person is good at all the abilities needed, and everyone can master at least one. The teacher would discuss with students all the abilities required by the task at hand. For instance, in a writing assignment, students might need to draw on creativity as well as reasoning, generalizations as well as specifics. The hope is that through discussing multiple abilities, the teacher will have replaced a generalized expectation of what is a "good" or "bad" writer with a more sophisticated understanding of the various competencies needed for a complex task. The goal, like Gardner's, is to replace the simple IQ-score view of intelligence with a much more complex vision.

Together, academic status and group work can either increase or decrease individual student learning. Even within a seemingly homogeneous classroom, some students simply have more status than others. Males, attractive students, and those who are perceived to be academically successful are among those often accorded "high status" by other students, and group work triggers students' awareness of academic status. Students with more status are more active in classrooms; they interact with their peers more and talk more than "low-status" students, and *that* affects learning outcomes. By the first few years of school, we are able to predict low achievers: those students who participate the least. The simple fact is that "those who talk more, learn more" (Cohen & Lotan, 1995, p. 100).

It is not hard to prove this point. One study, in particular, showed the effects on students of perceived ability (Dembo & McAuliffe, 1987). The researchers administered a bogus problem-solving test and then informed students—incorrectly and randomly—of who had average or above-average problem-solving abilities. The students were told that the skills tested were relevant to an upcoming task. Those students who had been told they had above-average scores acted like high-status students in performing the task: they dominated group interactions, had more influence, and were more likely to be perceived as leaders than the low-status students. Because of assumptions of academic ability, the high-status student acts and, in fact, *becomes* more competent: "The net effect is a self-fulfilling prophecy . . ." (Cohen & Lotan, 1995, p. 101). Those who are seen as having more academic ability dominate those who are perceived as having less. Since those who dominate do most of the learning, it is important that teachers intervene in normal classroom interactions and see to it that all students play an active part in the learning process.

The second of Cohen and Lotan's (1995) interventions is that of assigning competencies. The premise is that the teacher's evaluation of a student carries a lot of weight and is a major influence on students' perceptions of themselves. It has been found, for instance, that students who receive positive feedback from a teacher are more likely to raise their hands and volunteer in class. In this treatment, the teacher is careful not to give unconditional praise. As she circulates among students who are working, she waits until she observes a student who shows evidence of a particular ability, and then she comments on the competence. "The feedback has to be public, highly specific, and valid . . ." (p. 103). Others in the class must find the praise believable and understand exactly what the student has done well and how it relates to the larger task. The effect of this intervention is that lower-status group members participate more in the group and have more influence. The positive effect also carries over into new classroom situations. By using interventions such as multiple abilities and assigning competencies to low-status students, teachers can really influence who contributes to group discussion and how much. In that way, teachers can create equal opportunities for learning for all of their students.

Collaborative writing lends itself well to discussions of multiple intelligences and multiple abilities. Writing is not a single ability; one may be good at some of its parts or most of them, but almost never all of them. Writing involves creativity, organizational ability, and skill in the mechanics of writing: grammar, usage, punctuation, and spelling. One of the real advantages of collaborative writing is that a writing group can utilize the skills and talents of all its members; it would be a waste not to. While students are involved in collaborative writing, the teacher can easily circulate and discreetly listen in on co-authoring sessions. Later, he can point out the strengths of various students so that they can appreciate the multiple talents of their classmates.

Co-authoring allows students to proceed from their strengths. If students understand this, they have a better chance of honoring every group member's contribution, whether it be generating ideas or knowing punctuation rules. But for students to honor the concept of multiple abilities, they must first know about it. Discussing multiple intelligences and multiple abilities with a class and intervening to see to it that various students are honored for their specific abilities makes it possible for students to interact more positively within groups. For students to learn, they must view themselves as capable of success. Confidence that one can contribute to some aspect of the writing task can help students see themselves as successful.

Making/Breaking Groups

When teachers mention co-authoring, students sometimes groan. Surely, some students would prefer never to write with others because they feel they will be hindered by other students or because they worry that this process will reveal their weaknesses. Despite these fears, I believe all students should participate in occasional co-authoring because so much of our educational experience is carried out in the individual and/or competitive mode, a learning style that is accommodated most of the time. Collaborative writing allows students with different ways of knowing a chance to experience an alternative. Some evidence exists that collaborative learning is an effective pedagogy for women and minorities (Belenky et al., 1986). Honoring this alternative learning style allows their voices to be heard.

Co-authoring groups accomplish many positive goals: they can allow students to know each other in new ways, can provide a real representation of audience, and can give students a rare glimpse of other minds working through the problems that arise in composing. If students realize they can learn new writing strategies by observing their peers, they can become aware of alternative processes. However, there are many potential problems that can undo the possibility of true collaboration. As a case study later in this monograph will show, when students dismiss the abilities of others in the group, the group loses the capacity to gain cognitively. Worse still, the group members who are "picked on" can suffer real emotional damage.

A common complaint about co-authoring groups is that members can have different levels of motivation, causing frustrations with working styles. Even with equal motivation, some students prefer working

in groups, while others resist it. Some don't feel secure about an assignment unless they are ahead of schedule, and others really do write better under pressure. Some students want to get right down to business,
and others need some time to "bond" by getting to know each other; to
more directed students, that can seem like rambling or wasting time.
These are legitimate differences and causes for genuine concern.

Since we know that some of these problems may arise, it is best
to bring up these issues at the outset and then talk about positive group
behaviors. One of the most critical factors for a successful group is trust.
Trust keeps a group focused so that the members can work toward a
mutual goal. Only if group members trust each other can they be free
from fear of ridicule; that feeling of safety allows co-authors to communicate efficiently and cooperate fully. If they trust one another, members
of a collaborative writing group are likely to compensate for each
other's weaknesses and count on each other's strengths because they
know the others in the group would be fair and would be willing to
help them. That, in turn, can improve the quality of the project because
with trust, members are likely to bring out the best in each other
(Larson & LaFasto, 1989). In order to build that trust, groups should
have some ground rules that apply to everyone in the class and should
also be able to establish some rules of their own. They should anticipate
problems, like one person dominating, and decide ahead of time what
they will do. Students can keep process journals of their co-authoring
experience in which to frame and express their concerns about real or
potential problems.

Focusing on the Process of Co-authoring/Modeling

Before collaborative writing can be valued, many assumptions of traditional writing instruction need to be reevaluated, especially those that
stress product over process. School writing often seems to be driven by
considerations of form. That is why students' first questions about a
writing assignment are commonly about length. Traditional attitudes
emphasize writing as testing rather than as work in progress, and declar-
ative knowledge (knowing *that*) rather than procedural knowledge
(knowing *how*) (Langer & Applebee, 1987). In fact, the very process of
writing has been underplayed in many American writing classrooms.
When students write together, the process and product come together,
but teachers have to help students "see" that process. For instance,
when they collaborate, students are being shown audience response,
but only if they are alerted to that fact can they be mindful of peer

response as they are getting it. Since metacognitive knowledge of writing has, by and large, been ignored in writing classrooms (Applebee, 1982), we need to remind students to learn not only from their peers, but also from their *own* processes and reactions.

Traditional ways of teaching writing isolate students in a subject that should stress interaction. "Not only are writers physically alone at their desks, but they are psychically alone, ostensibly talking to themselves . . ."(Maimon, 1979, p. 366). Because, in our culture, writing has been represented as a solitary activity and because school success or failure in writing has been interpreted as a sign of personal success or failure, students who will be writing together need to be given not only a rationale for co-authoring (discussed earlier), but also some models of co-authoring.

There are a number of ways that co-authors can function. In the business and professional worlds, where co-authors often represent different areas of expertise, each co-author may write a different part of the document. Less often, each member drafts separately, and then the group selects the best of each person's work, or the group drafts together, word by word (Ede & Lunsford, 1990; Morgan et al., 1987). School writing works somewhat differently. In one study of co-authoring, students were allowed to complete a co-authoring task any way they wished. The groups fell into three categories: the "chunk" model, in which writers divided the sections to be written; the "raisin bread" model, in which one writer incorporated parts of the work of several others; and the "blended" model, in which co-authors shared the writing task throughout. The "blended" format produced the most successful papers, although it took more time for students (Fleming, 1988). That blended format is the one I support as a tool for teaching writing and the one which I model for students, because by negotiating an entire text, students can externalize their own writing processes, come to know their own strengths, and observe the writing processes of others. In another study of secondary students co-authoring, all of the collaborative writing groups co-authored in a blended style. While the students were not told how to accomplish the co-authoring task, the process had been modeled for them in that style (Dale, 1992).

Even before discussing the co-authoring process, you might want to discuss group behaviors that contribute to positive collaborative experiences. Often, students who are successful solo writers worry about doing too much of the work. If those students understand a bit about group dynamics, they might approach things differently. For instance, they need to understand the importance of listening, which includes the obvious—such as not interrupting—and the less obvious—such as looking at the speaker (Gong & Dragga, 1995). Any group member is more likely to contribute if she or he feels heard. If the more individualistic writers do not listen to the others, they typically feel that they are doing all the work and do not understand the extent to which they have created the silences of the other group members.

We can teach our students other skills besides listening to help promote positive group behavior. For instance, some students need to learn to wait for responses from their peers. We can tell students about the concept of "wait time," so that they, too, can understand that not all people process their thoughts at the same rate, and that if we are willing to wait, literally, just a few seconds more, we will get better responses from those we are working with. Another suggestion is that students respond to each other's suggestions for text in specific ways. Rather than saying, "That's good," students can learn to say, "I can really see that" or "Now I know what you mean." If students want to improve on text suggestions, they might profit from targeted instruction on helpful responses, such as "I think we need a specific example to back up that idea" or "Who is 'they' in that sentence?" or "I don't know what you mean there."

Because students have few collaborative models of interaction, it is important to discuss the process, focusing on productive conflict and negotiation. Disagreement is productive, but only if it is about ideas and not about personalities. Students can model writing for each other by the simple act of initiating some aspect of the process (Daiute & Dalton, 1993): brainstorming about an idea, suggesting an organizational plan, starting a paragraph with a topic sentence, offering an example to illustrate a point, or suggesting how to "wrap up" the paper. In co-authoring groups, peers can help each other become aware of "inert" knowledge, knowledge students do not know they possess (Daiute & Dalton, 1993). In a ninth-grade group, one writer always started with suggestions for a narrative introduction, a "story" about characters who illustrated the point. When another group member asked her why she did that, she said, "Because I hate boring introductions." When I interviewed her two co-authoring colleagues later in the year and asked them if they remembered learning anything in collaborative writing groups, both said they learned to focus on introductions that were not boring (Dale, 1992).

Students really benefit from watching others co-author. One possibility is to ask another teacher to come into your class for part of a period and to co-author a short piece for the class. If the co-authoring session is videotaped or audiotaped, then it will be available as a model for other classes. When I was studying co-authoring in a ninth-grade classroom, the classroom teacher and I modeled co-authoring on two separate occasions, both of which were videotaped. The point of the first session was to show students our process of narrowing and focusing a topic, an awkward process in the best of circumstances (Dale, 1992). Modeling our co-authoring process was risky since the two of us had never before co-authored, but neither had the students whom we were asking to write together. It was useful for students to see two English teachers struggle to focus a topic, decide what to include, and negotiate text. The class took some delight in the messiness of our process (Dale, 1992).

Another option is to ask student volunteers to co-author a short piece in front of the class. This session might also be videotaped. Before students do this, the class should discuss some guidelines, such as the necessity and value of every group member participating. The class can also decide on appropriate behavior for listening and for giving alternative ideas. They can take notes on what they think contributed positively to the co-authoring experience and what interfered with it. If students design their own class guidelines, they will be less likely to make moves that shut down the group and more likely to contribute positively.

Another way to focus students on their affective and cognitive co-authoring processes is to analyze a videotape of their initial collaboration session (Rogers & Horton, 1992) to see if they are working in productive ways. Because it is not often possible to get multiple video cameras set up, you can videotape five or ten minutes of each group so that the group members can see, if only briefly, how they function together. Another way to give students access to their own collaborations is to use multiple audio recorders while groups co-author during class. These are typically easier to access than videorecorders because of their size and cost. Even without the video component, students can learn from their collaborative writing session and will be interested in their own verbal contributions as well as those of their peers. Students can talk about how certain comments or evaluations made them feel. Time spent developing students' collaborative skills is probably time well invested.

Collaborative Exercises

Before students write together formally, it helps to engage them in activities that promote trust and that foreground the values of collaboration. Elizabeth Cohen, in *Designing Groupwork* (1986), describes several activities that might work for collaborative writing groups. One activity is to give each group member a bag with one portion of the pieces of a jigsaw puzzle which the group must complete without the benefit of the picture. The students may talk, but a basic rule is that each group member must contribute. Cohen also gives a detailed description of a frequently used cooperative-training exercise called "Broken Circles," in which each group member is given parts of a cardboard circle; the group "wins" when each member has a complete circle. The "hitch" is that the pieces can be obtained only by giving, not by taking. After such an activity, a teacher would link the experiences of students in a general cooperative exercise to the more specific task of writing with others.

To get students accustomed to writing together, have them complete several writing exercises and write several short pieces together in assignments that will not be evaluated or at least not heavily evaluated. By switching group members on each of these short writing exercises, students can get used to a variety of co-authors. After any of the exercises, students might write in their journals about the experience: how they liked working with others, how responsibility was divided, what they learned about their own strengths as writers, etc. The journals, then, can become the basis of whole-class discussion. The following collaborative writing exercises and activities might be helpful:

- Students can work together to catch and correct errors in spelling, punctuation, or usage. Give students a piece of student writing that needs some mechanical help and have students correct the errors. You might use a series of "Daily Oral Language" sentences (Vail & Papenfuss, 1989), if you have those available. Have students keep track of who knows specific areas of grammar and usage so that the class develops "specialists," such as someone who knows comma rules and someone who spells well. Those students can be resources for others in the class.

- Students can practice working together on aspects of writing such as coherence. Give each group a piece of student writing with coherence problems. Have them revise that piece.

- Cut up a paragraph into its sentences and have the group put the sentences together in what they think is a coherent paragraph.

- Cut up a story or an essay into its paragraphs and have the group put the paragraphs together in what they think is a coherent story or essay.

- Students in groups of three or four can contribute all they know about co-authoring and write about it in a paragraph.

- Students in groups of three or four can analyze video- or audiotapes of themselves or another group co-authoring. They might focus on which kinds of comments or questions move a group forward and which shut it down.

- Students with the same family placement—oldest, middle, youngest, only—in groups of three or four write a short essay about the advantages and disadvantages of that position. Because each student contributes experiences, these papers are often rich in detail. This writing is better done as a one-time group exercise, since grouping by birth order during a semester might not work toward achieving balance.

- Ask students in groups to clear their desks and take out a piece of paper. Put a lemon drop on each student's desk. Ask the group to write a paragraph that describes each of the five senses as they see, hear, touch, smell, and taste the lemon drop. The other objective is to use as many comparisons as possible. This collaborative exercise can be used to introduce poetry as well as to introduce co-authoring.

The following exercises and activities would work well for a group that the teacher has established to exist for a set period of time, such as a quarter or semester. Once stable co-authoring groups have been established, the members need to learn a bit about each other and how each member functions in the group:

- Have each student in the group describe a past collaborative activity that occurred in or out of school and then discuss how that activity felt. After groups have talked, the whole class can discuss past experiences with collaboration and focus on what makes groups work and what interferes with group functioning.

- Have members of the stable group list what they think are their strengths as writers and what areas still need work and then share this information with one another. Through this activity, students can become really aware of "multiple abilities" and see that each group member has something to offer. This activity can also lead to a class discussion of the various skills and dispositions that make good writing happen. At the end of the term, have students add to their original lists their strengths and their areas of writing to work on. They should have a fairly realistic idea because co-authoring gives students feedback on their strengths and weaknesses.

- Have students record a conversation with one or two friends (with their permission) and write out part of the dialogue. Then each student analyzes what he or she contributed to the conversation and what the other friend(s) contributed.

Students should ask themselves if the conversation was balanced or if one of the parties talked more (Gong & Dragga, 1995). Did one of the friends initiate all the topics of discussion or did all parties direct the conversation? This exercise could also be done in class, with a conversation occurring in their own co-authoring group.

- Have each student in the group write out about four statements that start with "I wish . . . ." When they are done, the group can combine these into a group "I Wish" poem. Kirby and Liner (1988) suggest this activity for a whole class, but it works very well for co-authoring groups because it lets group members know each other in a new and more connected way.

- After the permanent group has completed an activity such as the "I Wish" poem, they can come up with a name for their group. Having a name for a group can help to create a sense of solidarity.

ORGANIZING COLLABORATIVE WRITING IN THE CLASSROOM

Before students co-author in more or less permanent groups, the instructor needs to consider how to organize the groups and the writing. Inherent is the assumption that students need some direction and that the teacher as facilitator will provide it. That assumption is based not only on research (Daiute & Dalton, 1988; Dale, 1992; Ede & Lunsford, 1985), but also on my own classroom experiences. I refer to my own practice in this section of the monograph because few sources discuss the actual workings of collaborative writing groups in school settings.

Forming Groups

While it certainly is possible to let students form their own groups, students can gain more when a teacher places them in a group to further intentional goals. To achieve academic balance in a group, I do not look up students' past records to determine ability. That is in part because I believe each student deserves a fresh start and in part because previous research on collaborative writing shows co-authoring groups to be more effective when group members have a variety of viewpoints and skills (Ede and Lunsford, 1985) and when members differ in *performance*, but not necessarily in ability (Daiute & Dalton, 1988). The teacher's most important function is to prevent inequalities in groups; those imbalances in a group are of real concern because involvement is so closely linked to gains in learning (Cohen, 1994; Dale, 1996).

If students form their own groups, they tend to establish homogeneous ones. In one instance, when I allowed students in a ninth-grade class to select their own groups, all the groups ended up being same-gender ones. While there is nothing inherently wrong with same-gender groups, the members tend to be friends who may have similar skills and hold similar opinions. Such alliances can "blind the collaborators to opposing opinions or alternative ideas" (Gong & Dragga, 1995, p. 69). A group of white students might not be sensitive to the views of minorities, for instance, or a group of young women might not take into account the views of men. It is generally agreed that the more diversity, the better. Differences in socioeconomic and cultural background, as well as differences in ability, are positively associated with successful group work as long as the ability differences are not too extreme (Daiute & Dalton, 1988, 1993; Johnson & Johnson, 1979; Perret-Clermont, 1980; Slavin, 1989). The more diverse the co-authors, the more likely it is that issues that arise will be examined from many perspectives. Furthermore, when students work with diverse peers, they become more competent at relating to and working with individuals whose cultural and ethnic backgrounds are different from their own (Johnson & Johnson, 1994).

While making groups diverse is generally agreed upon as a positive goal, a word of caution is in order. Some instructors are wary of students viewing each other as representatives of social categories rather than as individuals (Cohen, 1994; Miller, Brewer, & Edwards, 1985). Acknowledging that groups were constructed to include a social category calls attention to race or gender and implies that teachers—and by implication, other authority figures—make decisions on the basis of category membership. In order to avoid students being grouped on a racial, ethnic, or gender basis, some authors recommend grouping students randomly (Miller & Harrington, 1990) or even alphabetically (Elbow & Belanoff, 1989). When I form groups of college students, I weigh heavily their class and work schedules; otherwise, getting together outside of class can be virtually impossible. One way to group students without categorizing them is to diversify the unique attributes each student brings to the writing project, such as understanding of genre, creativity, or facility with the mechanics of language (Hillebrand, 1994).

If possible, it is a good idea to begin collaborative writing early in the academic year. An early start allows students who do not know each other well to know each other as writers before they decide who is "smart" or who is a "good" writer. When students do not know each other's strengths, they can find their own individual areas of expertise. In fact, the strongest and most counterproductive force in groups is the status characteristic of initially perceived academic ability (Cohen, 1986; Lockheed, 1985; Meeker & Weitzel-O'Neill, 1985; Tammivaara, 1982). Forming groups at the beginning of the term is one way to counteract that powerful status characteristic if the school is so large that students do not all know one another very well.

One other consideration when forming groups relates to establishing criteria for positive group interaction on the basis of our own assumptions. We want students to work together, but we also want them to assert their individual views. When we have students from other cultures in our classes, we should be sensitive to their predilections, as Deborah Bosley (1993) points out. Because we know positive cognitive conflict leads to better writing, we encourage it, yet not all cultures can assert a point comfortably. Many Native Americans, for instance, believe that arguing one's own position is rude and disrupts group harmony. As Americans, we value specificity and directness, but that is difficult for many Asian students who are used to relying on context or nonverbal cues. We value lean prose with reasoned tones, but Middle Easterners often value hyperbole, and verbosity is considered an asset. As native speakers and writers of English, we are accustomed to starting with a general statement and then elaborating upon it, but Romance and Slavic writers tend to digress as a form of creativity. We want students to make the point; they are more likely to circumscribe it. The point is that when we teach students from other cultures, we need to be explicit about these issues. In talking openly about these differences, or role-playing them, or writing about them, we can broaden our own knowledge of the world and that of our students and at the same time head off possible cultural clashes.

At a much more logistical level, we have to decide how large co-authoring groups should be. The size of the group is related both to reward and to effort (Slavin, 1980). The larger the group, the less the reward depends on an individual's performance or ability to influence other group members to do their best. In my own classroom, I put three students in a group. Groups of three are large enough to encourage discussion about ideas, organization, and phrasing and yet small enough for each student's contribution to matter.

Providing Time

Just forming a co-authoring group does not create a sense of solidarity; it takes time to develop "groupness." That is one reason students should be allowed to work together on collaborative exercises before they are jointly responsible for writing a paper. If writing teachers do not provide enough time for students to write together, they are, in fact, discouraging authentic interaction: "[T]rue collaboration takes time— time to get to know each other, time to build trust within the group, time to wonder together" (Ervin & Fox, 1994, p. 64).

Since collaborative writing takes time, that time must be provided for students. When individuals write, their ideas percolate while they are doing other things, but collaborative writers do most of their thinking on the spot and with their group. It would save some class time if the teacher assigned the general topic or if groups met to determine a general topic at least a day before the co-authoring groups were to begin. That way, students would have time to consider the topic and have a base from which to start discussing. Kahn, Walter, and Johannessen (1984) point out that if students are given time to think before the group meets, they are less likely to sit and stare at each other at the beginning of the session.

In my 1992 study of ninth graders co-authoring, the students were given three consecutive class periods to complete an expository writing assignment. While a five-paragraph theme was never mentioned, that is approximately the genre in which students wrote. The three days were not sufficient for students to finish a draft that was really polished by their standards or mine. An extra day would have been desirable. It takes time for students to plan and negotiate throughout the writing process. I have always felt that co-authoring time is time well spent, given the range of learning possible.

Primary-Writer System

A central concern for many teachers and students is the "who-does-the-most-work" issue. That issue is built into the primary-writer format I use and relates to the number of students in a group. When I first started having students write together, groups turned in drafts so messy that they could not be read. What was preventing good work from being completed was neither the quality of the co-authoring discussions nor the ability of students to plan or revise. Rather, it was the lack of attention to logistical details: getting writing revised and edited so that it could be turned in. When groups did successfully complete a co-authored assignment, it seemed one person went the extra mile. That person might have taken notes during discussions, made copies of the joint draft, or compiled onto one copy the changes that other members had made verbally or on individual copies of a draft.

On the basis of that observation, I started a primary-writer format. This format spans the course of a semester. There are as many students in a co-authoring group as there are collaborative projects I intend to assign, and the primary writer shifts with each project. For instance, if I wanted to incorporate three collaborative writing assignments in a given semester, I would put three members in each group so that each would have the opportunity to be primary writer for one writing assignment. Although all of the students contribute to the writing project, the primary writer is responsible for making the process go smoothly, for going that extra mile. Each drafting day, the primary writer should have a copy of the draft-in-process available for each group member so that each member can read the draft and record changes to be made after discussion. By starting with a reading of that draft, students have a point of departure. If the primary writer does not keep the talk fairly focused on the writing, the paper will not be completed. However, some social talk is necessary for the group to cohere.

My insistence on multiple copies of the draft is based on personal experience. As I watched a group of tenth graders wrestle with trying to read a single copy of the group draft, I became convinced that each member must have a personal copy of the draft for real work to proceed. Because the cost of copying is an issue for many students, I make copies for the group if the primary writer gets the draft to me before class. Depending on the co-authoring process of a group, the primary writer might also synthesize material, finish a paragraph that was only half-written in class, clean up a messy draft, or key in the final draft. While there is no question that not every student will perform well as primary writer, the group puts the pressure on the student to be responsible.

Whether or not to assign primary writers for particular writing projects depends on your purpose and your knowledge of your students as writers. Often, I do not determine the order in which students will be primary writer. They can decide for themselves, and they often do so on the basis of their sports or rehearsal commitments. If I do determine the order, I start with a strong writer as primary writer and hope that a less-confident writer will have improved sufficiently to feel comfortable in the role by the end of the term. Sometimes the order is based on the nature or difficulty of the upcoming assignments or is designed to capitalize on particular student strengths. The more competitive students accept someone else being primarily responsible because each one has a turn, because the duties of the primary writer are fairly mechanical, and because they know they have input throughout the co-authoring process. There are, of course, other structures for these groups. For instance, if an instructor wanted to try only two collaborative assignments, she could form groups of four and have one student serve as primary writer for a rough draft and another student serve as primary writer for the final draft of each writing project.

Even though one student may be designated the primary writer, that is not the same as assigning roles such as recorder or encourager. When students discuss and plan projects in nonschool settings, they do so without being assigned roles, and it seems more authentic to me to structure school projects the same way. I prefer to give the authority to students themselves and encourage them to explore their own individual strengths. As a group, they can determine their own implicit roles, patterns, and rules. Successful collaborative writing allows "for the evolution of group norms and the negotiation of authority and responsibility" (Ede & Lunsford, 1990, p. 123).

Assignments

With the exception of suggesting a few collaborative exercises, there has been little mention of writing assignments in this monograph. The reason is that many kinds of assignments work well for co-authoring. Since so many English classrooms now involve writing workshops where students generate their own topics, a set assignment for an entire class is no longer necessarily the norm. Collaborative assignments can range from creative to persuasive writing. Each group could write a different assignment within the same or different genres. As with any writing, the more investment the students have with the topic, the more authentic the writing will be. For that reason, having each group decide on its own topic is certainly appropriate, but not necessary.

While there is not one kind of assignment that works best for a co-authored paper, certain guidelines apply (adapted from Rogers & Horton, 1992, pp. 143-144):

- Use an assignment that simulates a real-world situation.
- Give writers a group identity, such as members of a committee.
- Establish a diverse audience so that different perspectives can be honored.
- Center the assignment on conflicts between the writers and the audience to ensure a persuasive response.

Students must be active in defining the problem and the task. The negotiations necessary to do that involve students directly in problem finding as well as the problem-solving, critical-thinking skills teachers wish to foster.

Selecting topics that affect all students, topics that involve curriculum or school policy, for instance, gives students a good basis for collaboration because they are all stakeholders, and together they can develop meaningful positions. I often have students write about a controversial issue because the very nature of the topic demands that students analyze a topic thoroughly by reconciling divergent viewpoints, which in turn promotes cognitive conflict. When students disagree, "they are soon energetically practicing strategies for composing—challenging other viewpoints, answering objections from their audience, clarifying their reasoning, giving supporting evidence, and criticizing faulty logic" (Kahn, Walter, & Johannessen, 1984, p. 63).

Of course, all of that can go on while students are doing any kind of writing. At best, a co-authored assignment should "invite collaboration" (Ede & Lunsford, 1990, p. 123). That could play out in a variety of ways: students could have differing areas of expertise, the project could be too all-encompassing for one student to accomplish alone, or differing points of view could be valued. What is important to keep in mind is that when students write together, the focus is on the *process* and not the product.

Appendix A includes a number of assignments that work well for collaborative writing. Most of the assignments give just the co-authoring prompts, but the last few assignments include more elaboration in the form of models, customized variations, or collaborative writing edit sheets.

Focus on Process

Since attention to the writing process is a weakness for novice writers, collaborative writing, with its natural emphasis on process, can be a very effective means of teaching writing processes. Ideally, teachers should help students with unproductive writing processes by intervening in their writing to "untangle" these processes (Perl, 1979). But most writing instructors do not have the time to work so closely with their students on a regular basis. When they do confer with students, those conferences tend to be very short (Sperling, 1990). Collaborative writing offers an additional alternative. Since co-authoring groups work with each other through the entire writing process, they are a perfect means for "intervening in the individual's writing process, for working collectively to discover ideas, [and] for underscoring the writer's sense of audience" (DiPardo & Freedman, 1988, p. 123). While co-authoring, students can learn, through observation, more efficient ways to proceed which will help them gain control over their own writing processes.

The primary reason for students to collaborate in their writing is to learn strategies from each other, to explain their own thinking, and to take audience into account. Improved written expression may not be evident in the co-authored paper or in any one student's next few individual papers. But that is not a reason to give up on co-authoring as a learning strategy. Co-authoring puts the emphasis on the long-term goal of more rewarding writing processes. If we as writing teachers stress the short-term goal of the immediate product, then we very well may miss growth in student writers that is real, but not immediately apparent.

It is participating in the process of collaborative writing that can transform a student's ways of going about writing. In saying aloud what needs to be done next, students learn how to keep a writing process moving forward. As students explain what they do as they write, they "clarify their own processes for themselves" (Gere, 1990, p. 121). Teachers often complain that students fail to make connections between prewriting activities and the writing that these process activities were meant to support (Langer & Applebee, 1987), but in collaborative writing groups, students cannot miss the relationship between the process and the product. The function of co-authoring groups is to illustrate to students "how writing can evolve from half-formed thoughts to edited discourse," and to do so in a way that is "comprehensible enough to change behavior" (Clifford, 1981, p. 39).

WHAT HAPPENS IN THESE GROUPS?

So far, this account of collaborative writing has represented the voices of researchers and teachers who have taken advantage of co-authoring in their classrooms. What has been absent is the voices of students who have been involved in the process. In the next few sections of this monograph, I would like to bring in those voices to explain how these writing groups work. I will be referring primarily to ninth graders at a large, diverse midwestern high school where I participated in research on co-authoring. In the last sections of the monograph, I will refer to comments on co-authoring from college freshmen at a medium-sized state university in the Midwest.

The observations I make about how these groups operate do not often differentiate between the ninth-grade and college levels. My experience has been that collaborative writing works much the same way from middle school through adult writers. Although I have not worked with students younger than ninth grade, the literature in the field and the observations of elementary teachers who have used co-authoring lead me to believe that co-authoring operates similarly with younger students.

Overall, I think it's safe to say that younger students, those younger than college age, tend to learn the most about writing from each other because their writing processes are not yet clearly formed. Adults tend to have more rigid processes, ones that they are hesitant to abandon, even for one assignment, because they feel those processes have served them well. Perhaps most important, through co-authoring, they become aware of their own strategies and processes and learn to judge how effective they are. Once they realize that there are not right and wrong writing processes, older writers are more willing to integrate into their own writing the strategies of others. This is true especially when they are "stuck." Then they are eager to incorporate new strategies into their repertoires. When it comes to working with others, writers of all ages learn from their co-authoring experiences. When I feel that I need to differentiate between older and younger writers, I will do so, as I have done throughout this chapter in discussing groups, assignments, and evaluation.

Roles Based on Students' Strengths

In the ninth-grade study, the groups of three were assigned within the first few days of the academic year so that neither the students nor Carol, the classroom teacher, nor I would have many preconceived notions about who was "smart." We balanced gender and race in the groups and also tried to distribute the most outgoing students. That early in the year, we had only a small amount of student writing to go on, but we still tried to balance students with seemingly strong and weak mechanical skills.

The only model of co-authoring the students had was observing Carol and me when we co-authored for the class, and our input was quite balanced. The students' only instructions were to have all three of their voices represented. I was curious to see whether students would take on differentiated roles within the groups. Observing the groups and listening to the tapes of their writing conversations, it became clear to me that students soon found their own strengths and weaknesses and used *those* to divide writing responsibilities. When the students wrote journal entries about how they felt about writing, they were able to identify their areas of contribution. Joe, for instance, was well aware that he had weak mechanical skills. He wrote, "I'm horabl at speeling and dont know much about puncuations." Because of that, he never wrote the last draft of a paper but contributed wonderful examples as they were composing text aloud. In the same group, Alison insisted that she "hate[ed] boring beginnings" and loved to come up with narrative introductions, so the group always gave her primary responsibility for starting the paper.

In another group, Jenny was not in the habit of planning a paper before she wrote, so she would have Kelly write out a plan while they all talked through their ideas. Although Kelly responded early on that she didn't plan well, she found that Jenny and Frank were counting on her for that, so she took on that role. When I asked Jenny and Frank in interviews what they learned from others in the group, they both said that they had learned ways to brainstorm and organize. When it came time to write the first draft, Frank contributed most in the early planning stages because he considered himself their "idea person," and Jenny took responsibility for much of the phrasing because Kelly didn't "feel confident" about that.

If the point of co-authoring is the exchange of ideas and strategies, then introducing artificial roles takes away from meaningful interactions. It seems to me more natural and more fruitful for students to proceed from their strengths, so that they model their writing strengths for others and learn from the skills and strategies modeled by their peers. Just finding out what you are good at as a writer is a positive experience, and co-authoring is an excellent means of providing that experience. Another reason to let students define their own roles is that students need social as well as cognitive skills. In recognizing that everyone has strengths and weaknesses, students grow together socially and develop metacognitive awareness.

Leadership Style/Gender

When students are asked to do cooperative work in classrooms and are given no preparation for effective interaction, mixed-gender groups often run into problems with unwanted male dominance (Cohen, 1994). However, when students *do* have previous experience with co-authoring, this does not appear to be such a universal problem. In the study of ninth-grade co-authoring groups, no strong pattern emerged relating to gender (Dale, 1992). The groups spanned a continuum from having a very strong leader to having no leader at all. Since the role of recorder had not been assigned, I had been concerned that perhaps the secretarial duties of the group might be foisted disproportionately upon the females, but that did not happen.

The only pattern that was fairly consistent was when there was a leader: in almost all cases, the leader was of the dominant gender in the triad. For the ninth graders in this class, it seemed that a lone female could not direct the discourse for long if there were two males in the group or vice versa. Try as he might, Frank could not fool around enough to distract Kelly and Jenny for very long—even when he whistled the *1812 Overture.* When Ron and Andy did not want to be productive, Samantha had a hard time getting them to address the issues at hand.

While leadership was not related strongly to gender, stereotypical female speech patterns were evident when students wrote together, and *that* affected leadership style. Female-gendered speech patterns use a higher rate than males of hedges (*maybe*), intensifiers (*very*), tag questions (*Don't you think?*), and attention to politeness (Lakoff, 1973; Rubin & Greene, 1992). In the study of ninth graders, Samantha's speech best exemplifies these patterns. When the group was writing a paper about the availability of birth control for minors, the young men in the group, Andy and Ron, would suggest text in a straightforward way; Samantha, on the other hand, offered ideas and phrasing as questions:

> "Wouldn't it also tie in with them not being able to get their school work in?"

> "'Our main reason for birth control in school systems . . . .' Would that make sense?"

> "I keep thinking pills. Would this be the same? Does it make sense?"

If she did not suggest text as a question, then she often used the tag phrase "or something like that" after offering specific phrasing. Many of the young women used the same phrase. It seems that if one adds the phrase to a suggestion of text, one is less open to criticism; it is a way of allowing another group member to revise your phrasing without confrontation, a form of hedge.

Samantha's style was also different from the boys' when she tried to direct the group process:

> "Should we do a counterargument for that?"

> "Is this for parents?"

"Should we put another one [example] in?"

"Will they understand what you're talking about?"

This questioning pattern was common for the young women in the study. So while females were almost as likely as males to be in a leader or co-leader role, they handled that role differently from the boys, who had no trouble channeling the group process openly. The young women often determined the course of action and the text produced, but tended to cloak their leadership in questions and other nondirective language. I have seen these patterns of language and leadership play out in college as well as ninth-grade classes. While I am always a little dismayed to see gendered language patterns play out, I am heartened that there are young women in our classrooms who lead, nonetheless, in mixed-gender groups. Perhaps all young people need to have more models of female leadership who are direct and unapologetic.

Negative Focus on Surface Errors

One positive aspect of co-authoring is that students often learn mechanical skills from each other. In a major study of writing instruction, George Hillocks (1986) found that the biggest gains in quality of writing, including frequency of errors, occur when interaction is focused on development of ideas rather than correctness: "[G]rammar and mechanics may only be useful to writers when they are ready for it" (p. 225). In co-authoring groups, students *do* get mechanical advice when they are ready for it, "taught in a context of communicative need" (Sperling, 1993, p. 45). They are given the information about spelling, grammar, usage, or style as they are involved in making meaning and as they work toward a common goal.

However, when a group focuses too much on surface errors, the group shuts down and stops interacting purposefully, probably because some students perceive others as judging them in the same way they think a teacher or parent would. People like to write to express themselves but dislike writing if they feel they will be judged. Such feelings surfaced often in the ninth-grade co-authoring study. Tom, for instance, felt uncomfortable writing with a partner who judged his mechanical skills: "With Mark, I felt I was making mistakes. I couldn't spell or do punctuation. He'd bother me about that. He'd jump on me." Tom resented another student checking his writing to make sure it was "good enough."

The issue of emphasis on written correctness played out strongly in Dave, James, and Franny's group. Dave's response to how he felt about writing was typical of the ninth graders in the study. Early in the semester he had written: "I enjoy writing pretty much only when I can be the author and the teacher isn't over my shoulder the whole time telling me what to do." He worked well with James until James took on a teacherly tone, particularly in regard to Dave's weaknesses in spelling: "Watch this. Watch my sentence. It is *en*couraging." Dave replied: "Forget it. It doesn't matter." James made other teacher-like comments: "No. You can't start a sentence with *because.*" The tension got heavier when they argued back and forth for twenty-seven conversational turns, debating the spelling of *pregnancies.* Such conflict over surface errors is nonproductive. Dave maintained his pride by arguing with James to prevent a teacher-student hierarchy. But the time it took and the hostility it created turned a formerly effective group into an ineffective one.

Since so many students are uncomfortable when they feel their writing is being judged by another student, writing teachers who employ co-authoring groups need to be explicit about the negative effect a judgmental tone will have on the group. We need to convince students that blaming another group member for weak mechanical skills is counterproductive. If we frame the issue in terms of multiple skills, students may see co-authoring as a process of discovering and then utilize each student's strengths. Some students are excellent spellers and others punctuate effortlessly. Still others organize well or come up with good details or have a flair for phrasing. This mental habit of valuing different talents and then using various skills to accomplish a goal is a valuable one for many of the challenges students will face both in and out of school.

FACTORS THAT AFFECT THE SUCCESS OF CO-AUTHORING GROUPS

Because so many teachers are puzzled about what makes writing groups successful or not, I focused on that issue in studying ninth-grade co-authors. The meaning of success is important to define here since that word means such different things, depending on one's perspective. In this situation, Carol and I determined success as most teachers would, on the basis of observation. We observed all of the groups and overheard parts of their co-authoring discourse and then decided which groups seemed to function the best on the basis of positive engagement with each other and the writing task. We did not determine success solely on the basis of the collaborative paper the students produced, since my contention is that the real value of co-authoring lies in the interaction, not in the product.

Engagement

Because, when students write together, it is their verbal communications that generate content and promote learning, a high level of engagement is a critical factor in successful co-authoring. In the ninth-grade study of collaborative writing, co-authoring did seem to foster engagement; students were involved with each other and the emergent text (Dale, 1992). Students in the most successful group were animated in their discussions with each other and often exchanged conversational turns. Productive co-authors worked together on elaborating strands of ideas and were willing to create text aloud and modify their own thinking. When students co-author, sentences are often started by one student and completed by another, a sign of real engagement with literacy. When Heap (1989) observed first graders writing together, he noted that "students spoke, listened, wrote, and read" (p. 283). He points out that the oral writing involved in co-authoring is particularly useful in classrooms where some of the children are nonnative speakers of English. By hearing text as it is composed, children can learn language patterns as well as ways of approaching the organization of the paper.

It is simultaneous collaboration that leads to the most engagement, so it is important that students not break the writing task into parts and parcel it out. They should all share in the decisions involved in creating the text-in-process. When students do write together, you hear lots of talking and thinking aloud about ideas and phrasing for the writing. Students initiate ideas and contest them, which allows for reflective as well as generative thinking (Daiute & Dalton, 1993). However, not all of the talk about the writing task gets written down, and that can be a problem. If students do not get enough written down, they do not get sufficient credit for their efforts because the paper they produce will lack development. Perhaps discussing what to write down should be part of preparatory discussion.

Teachers often worry that students who write together will spend most of their time "off task." However, this is not borne out by current research. In studies conducted in first, third, fourth, and ninth grades, student talk during co-authoring was typically found to be very task oriented (Dale, 1994b; Heap, 1989). For the ninth graders studied, students in co-authoring groups averaged only 8 percent of their talk "off task." That amount of social talk does not seem problematic; students probably need some time to "bond" in a way that will make their oral writing flow. Although it may be unsettling to accept that some co-authoring talk will be on topics other than the writing, the situation is not so different from that in traditional classrooms. When students sit quietly while a teacher talks, there may be only the illusion that all students are fully engaged. In fact, *engagement* is perhaps a better term than *on task* to describe a student's relationship with learning.

Cognitive Conflict

Productive cognitive conflict is a major factor in determining the success of any co-authoring group; it is part of the process of effectively negotiating collaboratively written text. Collaborative writing is well suited to promote cognitive conflict since it involves social interactions which must lead to consensus. It is important that we differentiate substantive conflict—differences related to ideas and phrasing—and affective conflict—differences based on personality. As the next section will show, affective conflict can incapacitate a group, while cognitive conflict fuels a group. We need to teach students how to honor alternative viewpoints gracefully and perhaps even modify their own points of view.

Groups of co-authors often try to avoid conflict because it feels uncomfortable; that leads them to make decisions that go against their best judgments. A group cannot do its best if it rushes to consensus or seizes on the first idea presented without adequate discussion. All groups have at least one influential member. In effective groups, that person encourages all members to offer their opinions and to evaluate alternatives. In ineffective groups, the influential person accepts assumptions unquestioningly (Warburton, 1987) or phrasing uncritically. It seems obvious that a group which merely agreed to suggested text would be less involved and probably would produce weaker writing than a group that challenged each other's ideas so that the speaker would have to clarify reasoning and support ideas. Although even polite disagreement is uncomfortable for many students, we need to encourage it and help students to understand that groups that function well often have conflicting opinions. Cognitive conflict is key to the problem-solving process; it gives its members a broader understanding of the nature of the problem or issue, generates alternative ideas, and maintains interest and involvement (Warburton, 1987).

The transcripts of ninth graders co-authoring show cognitive conflict being played out. The group members whose dialogue I shall use as an example were composing the end of their paper by tying it into the ideas of their narrative introduction about "Tim" and "Jill." By offering alternative ideas, they forced each other to clarify their points:

> *Michael:* If birth control was made available to Tim and Jill, their lives would have been much different.
>
> *Rasheeta:* Or say the outcome could have been different.
>
> *Michael:* The outcome?
>
> *Rasheeta:* Yeah, because she wouldn't have been pregnant. That *was* the outcome.
>
> *Teresa:* Or she'd have less of a chance of being pregnant. You have to *use* birth control.
>
> *Rasheeta:* Outcomes. Yeah, I know.
>
> *Michael:* Outcome . . .
>
> *Teresa:* . . . of the situation might be different.

This group, the most successful in the study, engaged in cognitive conflict three times more often than the group which was judged as the least successful. I was curious about how aware students were of conflict in their groups and how they felt about it. The results of a questionnaire showed students to be highly aware that they often disagreed about ideas and phrasing. Interviews let me know how they felt about that. One group's responses are typical and explain why productive conflict elicits substantive engagement. Andy said: "By disagreeing, we thought of other solutions." Ron offered a similar opinion: "Disagreeing is good 'cause you figure out the best ideas." Samantha, the third member of that group, concurred that disagreeing "wasn't bad" and that it got resolved "because one of us always kept pushing."

It is not surprising that so much evidence points to a link between cognitive conflict and learning because substantive conflict engages students in reflective thinking. It forces them to legitimize their arguments and their language choices to a greater extent than they might when writing alone. When we teach writing in a social context, we must help students overcome the notion that co-authoring is "a cooperative activity that preclude[s] conflict" (Burnett, 1994a, p. 238) and explicitly teach them productive ways to disagree.

Social/Power Issues

The success of co-authoring groups is often determined by issues of status. Only groups in which students respect each other and in which all members' input is valued can function truly effectively. While issues of power and marginalization are implicit in any group work, they are heightened in collaborative writing groups for two reasons. First, students are ego involved in their writing. It is an expression of who they are and what they know. Second, the collaborative product forces a joint assessment which some students find threatening. Because of that, students have a greater reason to be invested in the outcome and fight for control of the group.

In collaborative writing, words do not just come together. It is people who come into contact through the medium of words; what students write is the product of their social interactions. If those interactions fail, if student disagreement is over persons and not ideas, then the group cannot proceed and will therefore reap none of the cognitive benefits. In the study of ninth graders being used here as an example (Dale, 1992, 1994b), the factor that most directly affected the success of a group is whether they made negative personal statements. The most successful group made no disparaging remarks about each other, while the least successful group made personal, negative comments in 8 percent of all conversational turns. Students sometimes discredited one another's ability ("How did you get in English [XX]?" "It's not like you're incapable, but . . . .") and resorted to name-calling ("retarded," "stupid"). When students are marginalized in their groups, they contribute less and therefore do not gain as much; it is what we express that we learn. In that way, social factors have a tremendous effect on cognitive ones. One simply learns less from listening to than from participating in an academic activity.

Teachers form groups, in part, to minimize power relations, to be facilitators rather than givers of knowledge, and to allow students to learn from each other. Teachers want students to be safe in their classrooms and safe in the groups within those classrooms, but just putting students in groups does not necessarily achieve that. As has already been mentioned, groups do not function well when one student adopts an authoritarian stance about procedure, mechanics, or text content. That will be seen again in a case study of one group that suffered the effects of power and marginalization. Even though this dysfunctional group did not succeed in co-authoring, we have much to learn from its members.

The primary reason this group functioned so poorly was that Mark established a voice that was dominant and counterproductive, the worst possible model of teacher voice. He felt free to insult the others and took on the role of inquisitor. In doing so, Mark silenced Sheri and intimidated Tom. He asked quiz questions rather than authentic ones, perverting the very strength of group talk (Nystrand & Gamoran, 1991). Most students in groups ask what they genuinely need to know, rather than use questions to establish hierarchy. Early in the discussion, when Mark was solic-

iting ideas, he badgered Sheri for her contribution. He was so intent
on grilling her that he didn't even seek Tom's input: "Tom, Sheri's
going to come up with the next idea. Why, Sheri, next reason? So you
don't say we stole all of your ideas like you usually do." Sheri gave a
reason, and when Tom tried to say something, Mark cut him off: "Shut
up, Tom. See if Sheri can think of something." Mark played teacher not
only by quizzing the others, but also by giving most of the directives.
His vision of teacher talk, however, was a perversion of classroom
management. He referred to himself in the third person: "Mark's got
his thought, but Mark wants to hear what other people say first."
Mark seemed to be trying out yet another teaching strategy—waiting
until the students found answers for themselves. But in the context of
a cooperative group, this strategy was not only high-handed, but also
counterproductive.

Mark picked on Tom as well, particularly about his competence
as a writer. After Tom read back their opening paragraph, he said,
"That's not a very strong opening," to which Mark replied, "That's why
it's your opening, because it's weak." As Tom continued to write that
day, Mark became increasingly critical of Tom's mechanical skills:

> *Mark:* Capital?
>
> *Tom:* I don't know why I capitalized it.
>
> *Mark:* He's dumb.
>
> *Tom:* Sorry.
>
> *Mark:* Tom, you, you've got the handwriting, but you have no
> idea of the rules of what to write. You leave spaces, lines
> between paragraphs, you do capitalization on every third
> word.

When I interviewed these ninth graders after the study, Tom was one of
the few who indicated he would rather write alone than write with a
judgmental peer.

The upshot of one student adopting a didactic role with other
group members is that discussion is less productive than most group
talk, each student responding to the "teacher" rather than responding
to each other. What occurred in this group is close to being a worst-case
scenario for collaborative writing groups. Luckily, most groups are far
more productive. But it is important that we as writing teachers are
aware of how negative social forces have the capacity to short-circuit
our best plans for creating positive learning environments. Once we
recognize the importance of the social interactions, we must emphasize
the abilities necessary to make collaborative writing work: the abilities

to distribute authority, to make other group members feel comfortable, and to involve all members in the work to be done (Locker, 1992).

EVALUATION

Writing programs which honor the social nature of writing presume (a) that writing and revising take time, (b) that there is no one correct way to write, and (c) that writers grow over time in a social context (Sperling, 1993). Any writing teacher who agrees with these assumptions must rethink traditional writing assessment, which has been overly driven by concerns with mechanical competence. All of the preceding assumptions play out in the way that teachers evaluate co-authoring. For instance, earlier in this monograph, *time* was mentioned as an important factor in collaborative writing. That is true in evaluation as well. Students must be given the time to engage in the process and communicate with each other and with the teacher. The second point, that there is no one correct way to write, is vital for students to understand as they evaluate each other; they must learn to accommodate different kinds of individual contributions. The third point, that students grow over time in a social context for writing, is one that directs us to valuing the processes students go through over valuing the collaborative product alone.

I do not want to give the impression that collaboratively written papers are not as good as individually written ones. In both ninth-grade and college freshman settings, I have found co-authored papers to be at least as good, if not better, than the average solo paper. Another recent study of co-authoring reported that "the final essays were far superior" to those written on the same assignment by the students who were writing alone. "They were not only better developed but showed a more thoughtful analysis . . ." (Hillebrand, 1994, p. 71). The point, then, is not that the quality of the papers is inferior, but that evaluating *only* the paper is not sufficient. When students are assessed by the jointly written product, without taking into account individual contributions, there is little incentive for students to work on the group writing process or make significant contributions to discussion. If there is a real dichotomy between the communal values of co-authoring and what is perceived as a competitive evaluation system, then students frequently complain about unfair division of labor and responsibility for the written product (Beard, Rymer, & Williams, 1989; Bosley, 1990).

Basis for Evaluation

The question, then, is, on what basis can co-authored work be fairly assessed? Writing instructors have many options in evaluating co-authoring. All of the evaluative choices include a teacher's input, which is established by reading the paper and other supporting materials, perhaps observing students at work, and counting students' input about their own contributions and those of their partners. I establish approximately 50 percent of the grade on the co-authored paper and 50 percent on the individual grade; that grade, in turn, is based on my assessment of a student's level of participation in discussion and text production, ability to deal with individual difference, and accessibility to others in the group. That last point is particularly important in college settings, where students must adjust their personal schedules to make co-authoring a priority.

Instructors of business students at a large state university gave 50 percent of the grade for the group report, another 25 percent for oral interaction, and 25 percent for the composing process. The students surveyed felt that this system was fair; they felt that each student pulled his or her own weight and each worked harder than when co-authoring only for a group grade (Beard, Rymer, and Williams, 1989). Another pattern is to grade for the quality of the document itself, the contents of an individual journal or log, and peer and self-evaluation. In such a scenario, the authors use both private logs and logs that students share with each other as feedback (Morgan et al., 1987).

There is another view that must be taken into account. Deborah Bosley (1993) offers a word of warning about tensions that can be created in multicultural settings when individual and group grades are paired. Although research shows that those who contribute to groups ultimately gain, "evaluating students individually may undermine the collaborative experience by placing emphasis on competition" (p. 54). Bosley points out that while our culture believes intragroup competition increases productivity, other cultures believe it decreases productivity by creating dissonance. While I still believe in giving weight to individual contributions, I would discuss this issue with the class. Those from different cultures make different, but valued, contributions; evaluation is not a zero-sum game. Individual grades need not be competitive. In a group that functions well, all members would receive excellent individual assessments.

Establishing Individual Grades

While we have established the value of individual grades, we have not yet established how to arrive at those grades. I use journals for feedback along the way as well as at the end of the project. In addition, I have students fill out peer and self-evaluation forms for summative evaluation. Journals (or logs) allow a teacher to assess individual co-authors as well as to get a reading on how well a group is functioning. Journals may also be shared among group members, but I do not have students share unless they wish to, because many students find that practice threatening.

The journals I assign are not specific—that is, I do not make students follow a set form with a set length. I ask them to write a journal entry every time the group meets and to indicate who is there, the amount of time spent, what was accomplished, and how it was accomplished. I ask them to let me know how they feel about the project and about the distribution of work for it. These journals give students a vehicle to focus on and monitor group interactions as well as a way to vent frustration. Students are told to be prepared to submit the journals whenever they are called for; this discourages students from trying to remember the whole process at the end of the project.

So that students will know how to deal with conflicts that may arise, a teacher has to talk explicitly about how to deal with difficult situations, a specific form of conflict mediation. As with any such mediation, the students must identify the problem; focus on the problem, not the person; have an open mind and a respectful attitude; and take responsibility for their own actions. Teachers can help to create an open line of communication by asking group members to tell their writing partners one quality they appreciate about each person and one quality they would like each co-author to change regarding how that person functions in the group. This activity can be done in writing, or it can be structured as a discussion. Students might appreciate a member's ability to do research or willingness to do much of the keyboarding. Students might ask one student to try harder to attend all group meetings and another to listen more carefully to fellow group members. Some instructors have groups write out goals such as "We will decide on our topic by _____" or "We will challenge each other's ideas, but we will not be rude."

If an instructor learns of a conflict through a journal entry, then the instructor can intervene when it seems appropriate. An example of such a conflict might involve a student who suspects she takes too much control in a group. In my freshman composition class, for instance, Chelsea was aware that "sometimes I feel like I'm taking over. It's not because I'm a control freak or that I'm even doing it purposely. I just like to get done." Her co-author Lisa confided that Chelsea liked "to take control a lot. This was helpful in areas where I wasn't very strong, but in areas that I was quite sufficient in, I found it to be degrading. I didn't feel as though my ideas were looked at—just disregarded."

In a similar situation, Anne resented Brad's high-handedness: "My idea for the introduction was the only one of my ideas that was used. It seemed to me that every time I suggested something, it was shot down. I can handle criticism and rejection, but not rudeness." In these situations, the teacher can check in on a group in class or conference with individual members, stressing that each person's role is to help in solving the problem, but not to solve it for everyone else. Another intervention is through written feedback. I might have suggested to Lisa and Anne that they assert themselves more, and I might have written Chelsea a note in the margin of her journal asking that she give the others a chance, even though I know how much she "just like[s] to get done." Journals can provide a safety valve for the group and a way for the instructor to provide assistance without directing the group (Goldstein & Malone, 1985).

As summative assessment, students fill in self- and partner evaluation forms. While some instructors have students rank group members and grade each other on specific criteria such as accepting responsibility, contributing ideas, cooperating, helping to resolve conflict, or finishing tasks (Bosley, 1990), I leave the criteria more open because I do not want to limit possible areas of contribution. Rather than fill in forms, some instructors have the group collaborate to arrive at one grade for each member of the collaborative writing group (Morgan et al., 1987), but I prefer to have students respond in writing to their own and their partners' strengths and weaknesses over the course of the project.

The forms I use are included as Appendix B. I keep them short and easy to complete so that evaluation does not seem like an additional burden. Students have indicated that they appreciate having real input into their grades and those of their peers, and since students know from the outset that their co-authors will be evaluating them, they are probably a little more diligent and cooperative than they might have been without such measures. Students are quite fair about their own contributions and those of others. Celia wrote that she was "on time and very cooperative, but I do have a problem with accepting others' ideas if they differ from my own." Harrison wrote that "Mary was not that reliable, and she would not voice her ideas. But she did a good job of researching and organizing." Brent wrote that Sara "treated each idea proposed like a determined novelist," and a returning adult student took it all in stride by writing, "Sam was very cooperative. He could use some work on reliability and responsibility—young, I guess."

I have learned a great deal from my students about the cognitive and social demands and rewards of co-authoring. At the end of the self-evaluation, I ask students what they think they've learned about writing from this collaborative assignment and what they've learned about working in groups. Most of the responses to the question about writing indicate that collaborative writing helps students with their individual writing. Aspects of writing that are mentioned most often involve learning to plan and learning through feedback how to take audience into account. Many have indicated that they learned that writing can be fun, a "lesson" I don't underestimate. If writing can be more fun—or at least less intimidating—students may put more energy into their individual writing processes.

In response to the question, "What have you learned about working in groups from this assignment?" students have a lot to say; they often write comments in the margins and on the back of the page. Following are a few representative examples:

> "Getting consistent feedback is what helped me."

> "You get feedback right away, and if one person does not catch a problem, chances are, the other partners will."

> "Each person plays an important role. If one person fails, the whole group fails."

> "You need to listen to your partners and consider their ideas."

> "You have to be flexible, cooperative, and willing to compromise."

> "I have had to learn to get along with others and not feel the need to take over the paper myself."

> "I learned that it is easy to work in a group if you can discuss problems. I think it makes the paper better because each person has individual talents."

Including student self- and peer evaluation as part of a co-authoring grade allows students to have an individual voice within the confines of a collaborative activity. That is the reassurance many students need, especially those who have been trained to value largely individual efforts. Knowing that others will be evaluating them gives students incentive to work toward a shared goal, if they need such incentive. These evaluations also give the instructor a window into the workings of the co-authoring groups and means of assessing fairly.

BENEFITS OF COLLABORATIVE WRITING

When teachers socialize the writing process and include collaborative writing in their repertoires, they take advantage of the relationship between speaking, writing, and responding. Authentic learning can happen in a cooperative writing environment because some of the responsibility for learning shifts to the students themselves, so teachers can adjust their own focus. When students see each other as resources rather than competitors, instructors can concentrate on teaching concepts that involve higher-order thinking (Cohen, Lotan, & Leechor, 1989; Johnson & Johnson, 1994).

As teachers, we can learn a lot about our students as writers from watching co-authoring groups. When we observe them writing together, "we become more sensitive to where students *are* in their learning, rather than concentrating on where we think they *should be*" (Morgan et al., 1987, p. 25). If, through observation, we can become aware of student difficulties in social, rhetorical, or mechanical areas, we have the opportunity to address those problems explicitly in our instruction. We can delight in students solving writing problems together and catch a glimpse of their externalized thinking about writing.

It is this opening out of writing strategies for oneself and others that allows for the learning inherent in collaborative writing. It transforms the usually lonely endeavor of writing by reestablishing its social framework and demystifies the process at the same time. What makes writing so difficult for so many students is that they must "relinquish collaborative discourse, with its reciprocal prompting and cognitive cooperation, and go it alone" (Moffett, 1983, p. 87). When students write together, they learn by interacting with each other and with the text. Co-authoring allows for the face-to-face planning and revising that encourages the talk about writing so vital in learning to be a writer (Rogers & Horton, 1992). Through that talk, students become involved in the whole writing process, become better problem solvers, and develop a tolerance for others' opinions and learning styles (Morgan et al., 1987). By co-authoring, students can learn a variety of planning strategies from their peers (Dale, 1994a, 1994b), an important point since there is a positive relationship between planning and writing performance. On a national assessment, those students who planned more demonstrated higher average writing achievement than their peers who engaged in less frequent planning (Applebee et al., 1990).

The ninth-grade students whom I surveyed and interviewed indicated that what they most remember learning from collaborative writing was different ways to plan. More than 60 percent of them said they spent more time planning when co-authoring than when writing alone. Earlier in this chapter, I mentioned Kelly, Jenny, and Frank. It was from Kelly that both Jenny and Frank learned to brainstorm before writing. Jenny explained, "The group helped me to brainstorm better. Before I didn't plan much. Now I might be more open to ideas and that'll help me think better. I'll spend more time on it." Frank, too, learned to plan from Kelly. He said, "I learned about writing down your ideas before you write. I never did that before. Now I'd do that to get organized. It's better than making it up as you go along."

Other groups, too, learned to plan from each other. Dave and James created a lot of tension by arguing over mechanical concerns, but Dave did feel he learned "how others work on a writing assignment. I'd be more likely to plan more in the future before writing." He used a wonderful metaphor, a "spider web of ideas," to describe what can be seen when "you put down your ideas." It was from Samantha that Ron and Andy learned about planning. Ron conceived this new process in an interesting way. He said he learned to "slow down. . . . Usually I'd just write. Now I'll brainstorm and organize." Andy saw planning as an investment: "It pays off." What he liked best about co-authoring was learning "how other people do their papers. You can get new ideas on how to write."

Eight months after I had co-taught and researched collaborative writing with twenty-four ninth graders, I returned to ask students what they remembered learning, if anything, from co-authoring. Seventy-three percent of the students mentioned planning or brainstorming as something they learned about writing by writing together. It seems that when students learn from each other, that learning "sticks."

SUMMARY

In this chapter, the focus has been on the practices and dispositions that help to establish successful co-authoring communities. Let me highlight the major points. To make collaborative writing run smoothly, teachers of writing will want to do the following:

- Re-envision authority in the classroom.
- Understand group functioning.
- Understand the rationale for co-authoring, and explain it to students and their parents.
- Understand the multiple abilities involved in composing.
- Model co-authoring processes.
- Provide collaborative exercises.
- Organize collaborative writing in the classroom: form groups, provide time, consider a primary-writer system.
- Consider whether to make specific assignments or whether to give students freedom to choose topics.
- Focus on writing process over writing product.

This chapter also addresses the functioning of successful collaborative writing groups:

- Student roles should be based on students' strengths and leadership styles.
- Unless forewarned, students tend to shut down productive writing interactions by focusing on surface errors.
- The success of a group is affected by its degree of engagement, level of cognitive conflict, and any social/power issues.
- Evaluation is based on a combination of joint and individual assessments in which students have some input.

FINAL REFLECTIONS

Collaborative writing has been an integral part of my teaching life. Through its lens I can trace my own growth as a writing instructor, from assignment giver and error finder to facilitator of writing communities. I went from using co-authoring as a gimmick to save time spent grading to believing in the power of co-authoring toward promoting student growth.

This monograph comes at the end of a long process in which all of my learning about and from collaborative writing became the book

I wish I had had when I started experimenting with co-authoring. I have learned not only from my own experience, but also from the teachers with whom I have worked, from my students, ninth grade through college, and from the luxury of time to reflect on my experiences.

I have learned that the line between too much teacher input and too little is a fine line indeed. And over time I have leaned toward less teacher-generated structure so that students can recognize that their ideas and initiatives are of value. I have also learned never to underestimate how much the social factors in groups affect the cognitive ones. I now make it clear to my students that co-authoring involves mutual responsibility for "interpersonal as well as intellectual tasks" (Noddings, 1991, p. 168). I involve students in discussions about how groups should run, what makes them work well, and what can cause harm. The teacher's responsibility is to prepare herself and her students as well as possible for collaboration and then allow the students to have some authority. Our work at that point is to learn from our students and their interactions who they are as writers.

Through co-authoring, I have learned that classrooms work best as writing communities where students learn what they know and what they need to know and where students learn to appreciate their peers' differing areas of expertise. When students share ideas and writing strategies, they learn to see their peers as sources of knowledge rather than as competitors. Over time I have perceived my role as an instructor of literacy become broader and more political. Establishing caring and ethical communities of writers is important in offering students a paradigm for democratic living.

Co-authoring can transform classrooms. To include and honor multiple voices in the creation of knowledge is to democratize the educational process (Ervin & Fox, 1994), and co-authoring brings alive the multiple voices of students' minds by externalizing them. We must capitalize on those externalized voices to help students better understand the writing process and their own strategies as well as themselves and others.

Students need not write in a vacuum if we provide them with the opportunity to teach each other what they know about writing. Certainly, collaborative writing cannot teach all students to write well in all situations and should not be the only way that students write. But rather than work against the goals of individual writing instruction, co-authoring can work for them by allowing students to proceed from their own strengths. Few activities involve students more closely as readers and writers "than that of collaboratives working together to seek after, express, and clarify a unified message" (Sperling, 1993, p. 39). Collaborative writing engages students in a process of knowing, and that is what learning is all about.

Appendix A: Collaborative Writing Assignments 1–14

Ideally, the pedagogy of collaboration and co-authoring is based on a vision of student ownership of writing—and therefore of the topics which prompt students to write. In writing workshops all across the country, students write about issues in which they are interested, issues important to their exploration of self or to the needs and visions of the community. When several students are interested in a common topic, they may seek each other out as co-authors. However, I realize that neither writing nor collaboration always plays out that way. There is a wide range in writing instruction in this country, from open workshops to direct instruction on the modes of discourse, and co-authoring can work in all of these situations.

Those of you whose students always choose their own topics probably have no need for this appendix. But others of you may find that you are more comfortable assigning a topic or several topics, especially if co-authoring is new to your students, rather than having them start off by negotiating topic choices. The topics you have used successfully before will probably be equally successful as co-authoring topics. I started assigning collaborative writing in the seventies as the most traditional of teachers, so I know that co-authoring can work well in that environment as well as in more process-based, student-centered classrooms. The point is that you need not abandon your current curriculum in order to give students the opportunity to write together.

Assignments for co-authored pieces are no different from assignments for solo writers; some are student generated, some are class generated, and some are teacher generated. Assignments for groups of students can be creative, satirical, expository, or argumentative. They can be about old chestnut topics or current controversies; they can be about literature or popular culture, about work or sport or soap operas. They can be spontaneous or a result of careful research. Students can write together about virtually any topic they can write about alone.

With the idea that some of you might appreciate seeing a few topics I have used as co-authoring assignments, I have included several in this appendix. Assignments 1 through 10 are just prompts; no other apparatus is given (for additional focus, see Hillebrand, 1994, for number 8, and Gong & Dragga, 1995, for number 9). Assignment 11 offers a professional model of creative writing in a specific style, which groups of students are asked to imitate. That assignment can also be a warm-up exercise. Assignments 12 and 13 involve use of the library. I find that students appreciate the support offered by a collaborative assignment if they are feeling intimidated, and many young people feel intimidated by the library and its resources, especially at the beginning of the year. Number 13 includes a group walk-through edit sheet as well as the assignment sheet. This assignment asks students to write a short manual which explains to other students how to use a particular library resource such as an index or abstract. Another co-authoring group walks through the draft of the group's paper to see if it is clear enough to be useful to future cohorts of students. (I keep a file of these papers, and when students have trouble researching, I invite them to consult my now extensive file of process papers on the indexes and abstracts in our school's library.) The numbered assignment guidelines explain the assignment more fully.

The most involved assignment reproduced here is the last one, number 14. For this assignment, collaborative writing groups are cast as research teams for a fictional state legislator. Each team researches an issue currently before the state legislature. Reproduced here are the materials students would receive: the assignment (with places for due dates to be filled in after they're assigned); an explanation of the genre of political research reporting; a group strategy worksheet; an explanation sheet about case-study peer editing; an individual edit sheet; and a group project evaluation sheet. Also, as an additional resource, an explanation of the assignment, geared to teachers, precedes the materials for students.

1–10 Prompts for Collaborative Writing

1. Write about a school policy. Gather information about the current status of the policy and interview (in person or by telephone) a person who could influence that policy. Write a letter to the person or group with the power to change the policy. Define the issue before you make a responsible policy recommendation and back up your stance with good arguments geared to your chosen audience. Past groups have written about topics such as required study hall, condom distribution, and smoking areas.

2. Find a problem that you think exists in this school or within a school organization, and then write a letter to a school official which defines the problem, proposes a solution, and details the feasibility of that solution. Perhaps you think that the school needs more child care or that parking privileges should be distributed differently. You might want to suggest a way to introduce a new intermural sport, overcome crowding in the dorms, or propose a meal plan that suits the needs of more students. Several drafts must be edited by members of another group and turned in for approval. These must include a proposal, a progress report, and a final report.

3. Choose an issue that you know your classmates are talking about. Write a questionnaire and survey classmates about their attitudes on this particular issue. You may also conduct short interviews. On the basis of your survey results, try to characterize the views at your school. You may try the same assignment in the larger community if you prefer to go beyond the bounds of the school.

4. Name your generation. Support your stance with explanation and specific detail drawn from the experiences of all members of the group. If you prefer, you can write a paper which protests the labeling of your generation as Generation X. You must still include the experiences and points of view of all group members.

5. As a group, brainstorm and decide on one invention or innovation that has had a very significant effect on your lives. Go beyond the obvious effects and really dig for the ways in which the invention has changed the way we function in the world. For instance, the telephone obviously lets us communicate with those far away. But

if we push deeper, we also see that it allows us to live far away from our older relatives and extended family, which, in turn, affects the fabric of family life. Write an essay analyzing the various effects on our lives of the invention or innovation you have chosen.

6. Think of some phenomenon or trend in society such as our social behavior, our eating trends, our tastes in entertainment, our views on family and community, etc. Combine your experiences as a group to really explore the underlying causes of this trend or phenomenon. Organize your essay around *reasons why* this trend or phenomenon exists.

7. Write a piece which satirizes a phenomenon in society, a script which satirizes a TV sitcom, or a newspaper which satirizes "rags" such as the *National Enquirer*. Choose a subject which is very specific in its characteristics or format and which you all find mildly to very irritating.

8. Write a paper that analyzes one particular advertisement. Describe the ad's script and visual message. Go beyond the description to do further research. You might investigate the product or the company which produces it, the target audience for the ad, or the psychology which motivates the ad. Your group must also analyze the ad for its underlying social message and evaluate the ad's effectiveness.

9. As a group, decide on a movie you want to view and analyze. It is up to you whether you want to meet at a theater to see a recently released film or get together where a VCR is available and view a film on videotape. On the basis of your class discussions of movie reviews, your group should compose a movie review of the film you watch together.

10. This assignment focuses on connotation and slanted language and uses political cartoons as a visual prompt. Your instructor may bring to class a set of political cartoons from which co-authoring groups may choose, or students may bring to class political cartoons of their own choosing. The group's first task is to describe the cartoon in one or more paragraphs but to be absolutely objective. The reader should not know from the description the leanings of the group. Then, the group members will write a several-page description of the cartoon using language as slanted as they can. This will involve the careful use of attribution words, "snarled" for

"said," for instance, as well as attention to detail and to connotation. These short papers can also be presented orally to the class.

11 Creative Writing in a Specific Style

The following paragraph describes a subject in motion. Read the paragraph that follows very carefully, noticing how Ray Bradbury introduces his subject (a dinosaur), how he describes it, and how he ends:

> Out of the mist, one hundred yards away, came Tyrannosaurus Rex. . . .
>
> It came on great, oiled, resilient, striding legs. It towered thirty feet above half of the trees, a great evil god folding its delicate watchmaker's claws close to its oily reptilian chest. Each lower leg was a piston, a thousand pounds of white bone, sunk in thick ropes of muscle, sheathed over in a gleam of pebbled skin like the mail of a terrible warrior. Each thigh was a ton of meat, ivory, and steel mesh. And from the great breathing cage of the upper body those two delicate arms dangled in front, arms with hands which might pick up and examine men like toys, while the snake neck coiled. And the head itself, a ton of sculptured stone, lifted easily upon the sky. Its mouth gaped, exposing a fence of teeth like daggers. Its eyes rolled, ostrich eggs, empty of all expression save hunger. It closed its mouth in a dead grin. It ran, its pelvic bones crushing aside trees and bushes, its taloned feet clawing damp earth, leaving prints six inches deep wherever it settled its weight. It ran with a gliding ballet step, far too poised and balanced for its ten tons. It moved into a sunlit arena warily, its beautifully reptile hands feeling the air.
>
> —from "A Sound of Thunder" by Ray Bradbury (p. 94)

Note the following:

a. The total description is geared to a dominant impression. What is it?

b. The description starts with an overall view and then moves to specifics. At what point?

c. The description has a pattern from lower to upper body.

d. The animal is described before the action begins.

e. The action further helps to create the effect desired.

Suggested topic: any person, animal, or object in motion. You might try specific subjects such as the following:

■ a cat about to pounce

■ a racehorse thundering to the finish line

- a basketball player about to dunk

- a quarterback about to throw a pass

- a dancer leaping

- a race car

    . . . or many others

Reminders:

a. Pick a tone or dominant impression first. Use the word(s) your group has picked as your title.

b. To begin, imagine your figure in motion as though it were "frozen" in a moment of action (like one frame of a motion picture).

c. Introduce the subject to the scene.

d. Describe the subject part by part (following a logical pattern like top to bottom, front to back, etc.).

e. Let the action occur at the end; "unfreeze" the frame.

f. Choose all your words and images, being guided by the dominant impression.

g. Use as many images and figures of speech as possible.

h. Overdo!

Each person in your group is responsible for keeping in mind all the ground rules as you base your co-authored paragraph on the Bradbury model.

Co-authoring in the Classroom by Helen Dale © 1997 NCTE.

12 Using the Library for Collaborative Writing

If your school has a library exercise, or if your teacher has written one to acquaint students with the various resources in the library, the group members can complete the library exercise together and then write about the experience. Each group should do the library exercise before doing the more formalized writing assignment about the library.

13a Library Process Essay on Indexes and Abstracts

An assignment that works well collaboratively is the "library process paper." Its purpose is to teach you how to use indexes and abstracts in the library, indexes such as *Current Index to Journals in Education*, *General Science Index*, and *Social Sciences Index* and abstracts such as *Criminal Justice Abstracts*, *Psychological Abstracts*, and *Sociological Abstracts*, many of which exist in both paper and electronic formats. The assignment is to write a process paper explaining to another group of students how to use the index or abstract to find an article about a hypothetical topic.

Assignment Guidelines:

1. As a group, choose a bibliographic resource on the list, and together, do the needed research. Write and hand in one essay. Your audience for the essay is composed of students in next semester's class. The paper should be 3–6 typed pages.

2. The introductory paragraph should tell exactly where the resource is located in the library and how to find it. Give background on the resource. Indicate what type it is (index/abstract) and for what purpose you might use it in normal research.

3. The middle paragraphs should contain a chronological, step-by-step description of how to use the resource. Before you begin, choose a hypothetical topic that you might reasonably expect to find in this resource. Find references to that topic in your resource. Give a typical entry on the topic, explaining what the abbreviations and notes mean. Take one entry and actually find the article or information at your library. You must touch the article! Make sure you describe the process you used to locate the article or information. How did you know whether or not your library owned that journal? Once you locate the article, give a short summary of its contents.

4. In the concluding paragraph, comment on specific strengths and weaknesses of the resource. How effective is it as a resource in its subject area? How hard or easy is it to use? How clear or confusing is it to use in finding the article or information referred to?

Co-authoring in the Classroom by Helen Dale © 1997 NCTE.

13b Walk-Through Edit Sheet: Library Process Essay on Indexes and Abstracts

Names of writers of paper: _____

Names of editors: _____

Instructions to the editors: As you read the paper you were given, follow the steps as detailed below and answer the questions in the blanks provided, giving the writers specific feedback at any point where their paper needs to be clearer or more complete.

1. What is the name of the index or abstract?

2. Use the directions given in the paper to find the index in the library. Did the paper give you clear directions on how to find the index?

3. Is the general description of the resource clear?

4. Does the paper give a good indication of the types of topics for which you'd use this index? Comment.

5. Look closely at the chronological transitions. Are they clear enough?

6. What hypothetical topic have the writers chosen? _____
_____ . Using instructions given in the paper, find another article on the topic used by the writers. Copy the citation here.

7. Are the steps for using this index/abstract explained in enough detail? As you tried to use the index to answer question 6 above, were any instructions hard to follow?

8. Does the paper explain clearly, as well as illustrate, how to interpret all parts of the citation? Comment.

9a. Does the paper explain how to determine if an article is available in your library and, if so, where it is located? Using the instructions given in the paper, indicate below whether your library owns the article you cited in question 6. If so, give its location and format.

9b. Were any of these instructions hard to follow?

10. What special pitfalls did the paper alert you to watch out for?

11. Do the writers comment on the strengths and weaknesses of the index/abstract? Are those comments specific enough? Comment.

12. Is the style of the writing smooth? The sentences varied? The voice appropriate for the intended audience?

13. What did you as a group like best about this paper?

14. Make one suggestion the writers can use to improve this paper for their last draft.

14 Collaborative Case Study: Notes for Teachers

The most major assignment my students co-author is the "collaborative case study." The students are cast as research teams for a fictional state legislator, and each group researches a particular issue for that person. Since this project is such a large one, I explain to students that three areas of expertise need to be coordinated: research, generating text, and editing. I do not assign these as roles (for reasons I have detailed elsewhere in this manuscript), but students know that as a group, they are accountable for coordinating those efforts. As topics, I choose issues that have been—or are currently being—debated in the legislature: handgun control, lowering the drinking age, mandatory seat-belt and helmet laws, mandatory recycling of tires, domestic partnership privileges, term limits for politicians, legally assisted suicide for the terminally ill, the death penalty, welfare reform, "boot camp" for juvenile offenders, and year-round schooling, which I will use here as a sample assignment. Included in the following pages are the materials that the students in my class would receive:

a. a sample assignment

b. an explanation of research reports

c. a group research-strategy worksheet

d. an explanation of peer editing

e. an individual edit sheet

f. a project evaluation form

14a Collaborative Case Study:
Assignment Sheet

To: Chris Davidson
   Zach Smith
   Corrine Winters

From: Dale Stevens, Administrative Assistant to Assemblyperson Joseph

Re: Research report for Assemblyperson Joseph, 93rd Assembly District,
   Wisconsin

Situation: You have been hired as legislative interns to assist Assemblyperson Joseph in reviewing upcoming legislation. In the next session of the legislature, a bill will be introduced to require elementary and secondary schools to adopt a calendar which requires year-round schooling. Although Assemblyperson Joseph knows that year-round schooling is one of many educational reforms suggested across the United States, she lacks background on this issue and does not want to be swayed by emotion. Therefore, she is assigning to her research assistants the task of researching this issue and making a recommendation on how she should vote. This is only one of many issues she is examining, so your report must be concise. The complete research report must be read prior to the scheduling of this bill in committee on November __, 19__. Your report is therefore due at 1:00 p.m. on November __, 19__, the day before the committee meets.

———

The research report should be no longer than eight (8) double-spaced, typewritten pages. The works cited page and appendixes will not count toward the total length of the paper.

Due Dates:

_____   Individual search strategies should be completed.

_____   Group search-strategy proposal for the case study is due at the
            beginning of class.

_____ The rough draft of the case-study collaborative paper is due. The group must have 3 edit sheets and 3 copies of the draft. Today's class will be peer editing.

_____ The final draft of the case study is due at the beginning of class. The research report should be turned in enclosed in a folder with a pocket on each side. In the right side, put the final typed draft. Paper-clip the pages together—*do not staple.* Photocopies of sources should be in the left pocket, with all underlining, etc.

The paper should be presented in the following order: title page; outline, headed with a thesis (all Roman numerals and A's and B's should be full sentences); the text itself, with pages numbered and double-spaced; the works cited page, done in the correct form (follow the form in your handbook); and any appendixes you deem appropriate. Also in the right pocket, include the group edit sheet. *Note:* You must attach your group's response to the editors' recommendations on the back of the group edit sheet.

In the *left* side pocket, include the following:

- all rough drafts;
- all unused underlined articles;
- all unused bibliographic sources, rubber-banded together. On each of these bibliography cards, write a sentence explaining why that source was not used. Put your name on the back of the rubber-banded "deck."
- a comprehensive research log for the group. Indicate each step of the research process from the time your group began to analyze its topic. Include all individual research logs which reflect research done on this project. Your strategy is very important. Don't neglect this step.

_____ During this week, your group will be assigned a time to do a poster presentation that highlights your topic and explains your recommendation and how you reached that conclusion.

Co-authoring in the Classroom by Helen Dale © 1997 NCTE.

14b Collaborative Case Study: Research Report

The research report goes by many names: analytical report, position paper, opinion paper, or, simply, research report. No matter what name is used, a research report has two specific objectives:

(1) to present the findings of the research;

(2) to communicate the conclusions and recommendations.

Sources of Information:

Research reports utilize three basic sources of information. They are as follows:

1. *Personal and Professional Experience.* At this point in your life, most of you lack the background to use this as a major resource; however, personal experience and common sense should help you avoid making quantum leaps in judgment.

2. *Library Research.* Since more knowledge exists than any person can be expected to know, this is an essential element. Good research requires the ability to analyze a topic, the knowledge of a discipline's present stage of evolution, the ability to select appropriate research tools, and a means of evaluation for selecting the appropriate sources from those retrieved.

3. *Original Research.* Opinion polls, experiments, interviews, surveys, data analyses, etc., may be necessary when neither library material nor personal experience provides the answers. (*Note:* Library materials used as primary resources fit into this category. For example, you are doing research about raising the drinking age to twenty-one. Use of *Newsbank* establishes that legislation to reverse this decision is pending in fifteen states. Although no article states that "legislation is pending in fifteen states," you can certainly state that "an analysis of articles indexed in *Newsbank* demonstrates that no region of the United States remains untouched by this issue.")

Structure of the Report:

There is no single accepted structure for a research report since conclusions may be given either first or last. The order is usually determined by looking at both the audience for and the purpose of the report. You may choose to place the conclusions first for an audience of busy readers who are already informed about the topic. Yet, for an audience which needs persuasion, you may choose to lead these readers step-by-step to the final recommendations.

Although the placement of conclusions can vary, research reports have the following elements in common:

a. The *introduction* presents a general statement of the problem, gives a historical review of the subject, states the purpose of the report in one sentence, notes the scope and limitations of the report, and explains the order in which the topics will be presented.

b. The *body* includes an analysis of the various aspects of the problem and possible solutions to the overall problem. This section may be organized in either of the following ways: identifying a problem and proposing solutions to it or stating all problems in one section and then suggesting solutions and discussing their merits in another section. This latter approach is frequently less confusing.

   Borrowed material must be introduced by using parenthetical citations. Please note that much greater use is made of paraphrase than of direct quotation. Since the final conclusions should be your own, this portion should not include any direct quotations.

c. The *conclusion* summarizes the major points of the report, states the conclusions, and makes final recommendations for action.

d. The *works cited page* provides bibliographical citations for all borrowed material cited in the report. Occasionally, a list of citations for related material not cited in the report may be appended and headed as "For Additional Reading" or some other, similar heading.

e. *Graphics* (optional) may be in the form of tables, bar graphs, pie charts, line charts, organizational charts, flow charts, etc. They may be included in the body of the report or attached as appendixes. Graphics are introduced in the text by directing the reader to the appropriate illustration—for example, "The dramatic increase in the number of offshore drilling platforms (see Appendix A) substantiates the need for . . . ."

f. *Appendixes* (optional) provide supporting data for statements made in the text.

Co-authoring in the Classroom by Helen Dale © 1997 NCTE.

14c Collaborative Case Study: Group Strategy Worksheet

Names: _____

_____

_____

This sheet is intended to help you synthesize individual strategies into a comprehensive, preliminary plan that will assist the group in locating appropriate information on its topic in an organized and systematic manner. This comprehensive plan is particularly important since group members must coordinate their research in order to avoid either unnecessary duplication of work or totally overlooked sources. Don't expect to find information specifically on the events taking place in Wisconsin or even on a specific bill. Look at the general issue and what has happened in other states, regions, etc. You may also need to use statistical data and to draw your own conclusions:

1. List the broad topic.

2. Use *First Stop,* which is kept at the reference desk, to identify sources of background information. Look at the sources found in the individual strategies. Identify the two best sources of background material and list the titles, volume, and pages of background information as given in *First Stop.*

3. Which subject headings lead to books on your topic?

4. Which keywords are useful for finding books on your topic?

5. Which disciplines would you expect to be interested in this topic?

6. Consult your individual strategies and compare the results. Give the titles of periodical indexes and abstracts that were most useful in finding articles on your topic:

   Title:

   Subject headings which are useful:

   Title:

   Subject headings which are useful:

   Title:

   Subject headings which are useful:

   Title:

   Subject headings which are useful:

7. Did you locate any sources of statistics which might enhance your understanding of the issues surrounding your case-study topic? If so, give the title, page number, and call number of the item.

8. Which newspaper indexes have material on your topic?

   Title:

   Subject headings:

Title:

Subject headings:

9. Use Infotrac's *Expanded Academic Index* to locate an article on your topic. Provide the citation to the article you select.

10. Which indexes to U.S. documents have information on your topic?

    Title:

    Subject headings:

    Title:

    Subject headings:

11. Use the online catalog to search Wisconsin documents and list below three State of Wisconsin publications that may include useful information.

14d Collaborative Case Study: Peer Editing

When you do your peer editing of the case study, it is important that each member of the group begin by reading through the case you are editing and fill out an individual edit sheet.

Once each of you has completed the individual editing, discuss the case study as a group and reach a consensus on the strengths and weaknesses of the case study you are editing. This consensus forms the basis of what you will include on the group edit sheet.

Return all copies of the case study, all individual edit sheets, and the group edit sheet to the group whose work you edited. Be prepared to discuss any questions that group may have about your comments. (This is important and may need to be done outside of class.)

Once you have your group's edited case study and the edit sheets, you must read the comments and make any needed changes. Please take the suggestions seriously. Often, the problems a teacher spots in a paper are precisely the ones identified by the editors. If you do not believe the suggestions are valid, you should attach a written rationale for any major suggestion you choose to ignore.

When you turn in your final draft of the case study, you must attach the edited versions and the peer-group edit sheet.

14e Collaborative Case Study: Individual Edit Sheet

Writers: _____

Editor: _____

Quickly read through the paper on your own. Look for the following items and quickly jot down your initial comments and reactions. If you need to refer to a particular part of the paper, write down page and paragraph numbers.

1. Does the outline page state the recommendation as a thesis statement? _____. Is there a functional outline? _____.

2. Does the introduction present a historical review of the subject? _____. Does it state the purpose of the report succinctly? _____. And does it note the scope and limitations of the report? _____.

3. Is each problem clearly identified with enough detail so that you can understand the problem? Comment by paragraph number on any that aren't.

4. Are supporting reasons for the final recommendation stated clearly and discussed in detail? Comment by paragraph on any that aren't.

5. Are the opposing viewpoints acknowledged and briefly discussed? Comment by paragraph on any that aren't.

6. Are the reasoning and logic clear? Do they naturally lead to the final recommendation?

7. Are the major points summarized and the conclusions stated in the concluding paragraph(s) of the report? Indicate any that you believe are omitted.

8. Are the reasons for the final recommendation stated convincingly? Do they persuade you that the recommendation was the correct one?

9. Is the recommendation stated clearly?

10. Does the report maintain a single voice as opposed to sounding cobbled together?

11. Does the tone of the report lead the reader to conclude that an objective analysis was made before a conclusion was reached?

12. Is all borrowed information introduced? Is it introduced meaningfully?

13. Is all borrowed information documented (in parentheses)? Can you tell on which page of which source the material comes from?

14. If graphics or appendixes are included, are they introduced smoothly into the text? Are they meaningful? Are additional supporting data needed to clarify the recommendation?

15. What do you like best about this paper?

16. If the paper were yours, what one thing about it would you change?

17. Is the works cited page in correct form and the entries in alphabetical order?

14f Collaborative Case Study: Group Project Evaluation

Name: _____

A. Project Evaluation

1. Project title/topic:

2. The grade you expect this project to receive: _____. Explain why.

3. What are some significant ideas/facts/inferences you learned from this topic?

B. Group Evaluation (Be sure to evaluate your own performance in the group.)

1. Person #1 (Yourself): _____

   a. Strengths within this project:

   b. Weaknesses within this project:

   c. Comments:

2. Person #2: _____

    a. Strengths within this project:

    b. Weaknesses within this project:

    c. Comments:

3. Person #3: _____

    a. Strengths within this project:

    b. Weaknesses within this project:

    c. Comments:

Appendix B: Collaborative Writing Evaluation Forms

Collaborative Writing Self-Evaluation

Project: Name:

Date: Group #:

1. *Evaluate* yourself, commenting specifically on the following:

    a. *Identify* your contributions to the paper (e.g., providing ideas, research, typing, or strengths in planning, organizing, editing, etc.).

    b. Comment on the *quality* of your contribution.

    c. Comment on your strengths and weaknesses as a writing partner (e.g., reliability, cooperation, responsibility, etc.).

    d. Grade your overall contributions to the collaborative writing project. Circle 1, 2, 3, or 4:
        4 = excellent   3= good   2= fair   1 = unacceptable

2. What, if anything, would have made the process of writing this paper go more smoothly?

3. What, if anything, really went right? What did you like about the process?

4. What do you think you have learned about writing from this collaborative assignment?

5. What have you learned about working in groups from this assignment?

Collaborative Writing Partner Evaluation

Project: Name:

Date: Group #:

Please comment honestly and specifically on the contribution of
_____ (one partner's name).

1. *Identify* his/her contributions to the paper (e.g., providing ideas, research, typing, or strengths in planning, organizing, or editing, etc.).

2. Comment on the *quality* of his/her contributions.

3. Comment on the person's strengths and weaknesses as a writing partner (e.g., reliability, cooperation, responsibility, etc.).

4. Please grade this person's overall contributions to the collaborative writing project. Circle 1, 2, 3, or 4:
       4 = excellent   3 = good   2 = fair   1 = unacceptable

Works Cited

Applebee, A.N. (1982). Writing and learning in school settings. In M. Ny-strand (Ed.), *What writers know: The language, process, and structure of written discourse* (pp. 365–381). New York: Academic Press.

Applebee, A.N., Langer, J.A., Jenkins, L.B., Mullins, I.V.S., & Foertsch, M.A. (1990). *Learning to write in our nation's schools: Instruction and achievement in 1988 at grades 4, 8, and 12.* Princeton, NJ: National Assessment of Educational Progress and Educational Testing Service.

Ashton-Jones, E., & Thomas, D.K. (1990). Composition, collaboration, and women's ways of knowing: A conversation with Mary Belenky. *Journal of Advanced Composition, 10,* 275–292.

Bakhtin, M.M. (1981). *The dialogic imagination.* Ed. M. Holquist. (Trans. C. Emerson & M. Holquist). Austin: University of Texas Press.

Bargh, J.A., & Schul, Y. (1980). On the cognitive benefits of teaching. *Journal of Educational Psychology, 72,* 593–604.

Beard, J.D., Rymer, J., & Williams, D.W. (1989). An assessment system for collaborative-writing groups: Theory and empirical evaluation. *Journal of Business and Technical Communication, 3,* 29–51.

Belenky, M., Clinchy, B., Goldberger, N., & Tarule, J. (1986). *Women's ways of knowing.* New York: Basic Books.

Bereiter, C., & Scardamalia, M. (1982). From conversation to composition: The role of instruction in a developmental process. In R. Glaser (Ed.), *Advances in instructional psychology, vol. 2* (pp. 1–64). Hillsdale, NJ: Erlbaum.

Bereiter, C., & Scardamalia, M. (1987). *The psychology of written composition.* Hillsdale, NJ: Erlbaum.

Bizzell, P. (1986). Composing processes: An overview. In A.R. Petrosky & D. Bartholomae (Eds.), *The teaching of writing. Eighty-fifth yearbook of the National Society for the Study of Education, part II* (pp. 49–70). Chicago: University of Chicago Press.

Bosley, D.S. (1990). Individual evaluation in a collaborative report project. *Technical Communication, 37,* 160–164.

Bosley, D.S. (1993). Cross-cultural collaboration: Whose culture is it, anyway? *Technical Communication Quarterly, 2*(1), 51–62.

Bossert, S.T. (1988). Cooperative activities in the classroom. *Review of Research in Education, 15,* 225–250.

Bouton, C., & Garth, R.Y. (1983). Students in learning groups: Active learning through conversation. In C. Bouton & R.Y. Garth (Eds.), *Learning in groups. New directions for teaching and learning, no. 14* (pp. 73–82). San Francisco: Jossey-Bass.

Bradbury, R. (1953). A sound of thunder. In *The golden apples of the sun* (pp. 88–99). New York: Bantam.

Bridwell, L.S. (1980). Revising strategies in twelfth-grade students' transactional writing. *Research in the Teaching of English, 14*(3), 197–222.

Britton, J., Burgess, A., Martin, N., McLeod, A., & Rosen, H. (1975). *The development of writing abilities, 11–18.* London: Macmillan Education.

Brown, A.L., & Palincsar, A.S. (1989). Guided, cooperative learning and individual knowledge acquisition. In L.B. Resnick (Ed.), *Knowing, learning, and instruction: Essays in honor of Robert Glaser* (pp. 393–451). Hillsdale, NJ: Lawrence.

Bruffee, K.A. (1984). Collaborative learning and the "conversation of mankind." *College English, 46*(7), 635–652.

Bruffee, K.A. (1985). *A short course in writing* (3rd ed.). Boston: Little, Brown.

Burnett, R.E. (1992). Characterizing conflict in collaborative relationships: The nature of decision making during co-authoring. In C. Thralles & N. Blyer (Eds.), *The social perspective in professional communication* (pp. 144–162). Newbury Park, CA: Sage.

Burnett, R.E. (1994a). Productive and unproductive conflict in collaboration. In L. Flower, D.L. Wallace, L. Norris, & R.E. Burnett (Eds.), *Making thinking visible: Writing, collaborative planning, and classroom inquiry* (pp. 237–242). Urbana, IL: National Council of Teachers of English.

Burnett, R.E. (1994b, November). Classroom collaboration: Encouraging conflict and consensus. Paper presented at the annual convention of the National Council of Teachers of English, Orlando, FL.

Clifford, J. (1981). Composing in stages: The effects of a collaborative pedagogy. *Research in the Teaching of English, 15*(1), 37–53.

Cohen, E.G. (1986). *Designing groupwork.* New York: Teachers College Press.

Cohen, E.G. (1994). Restructuring the classroom: Conditions for productive small groups. *Review of Educational Research, 64*(1), 1–35.

Cohen, E.G., & Lotan, R.A. (1995). Productive equal-status interaction in the heterogeneous classroom. *American Educational Research Journal, 32*(1), 99–120.

Cohen, E.G., Lotan, R.A., & Leechor, C. (1989). Can classrooms learn? *Sociology of Education, 62,* 75–94.

Daiute, C. (1986). Do 1 and 1 make 2? Patterns of influence by collaborative authors. *Written Communication, 3*(3), 382–408.

Daiute, C., & Dalton, B. (1988). Let's brighten it up a bit: Collaboration and cognition in writing. In B.A. Rafoth & D.L. Rubin (Eds.), *The social construction of written communication* (pp. 249–269). Norwood, NJ: Ablex.

Daiute, C., & Dalton, B. (1993). Collaboration between children learning to write: Can novices be masters? *Cognition and Instruction, 10*(4), 281–333.

Dale, H. (1992). Collaborative writing: A singular we. Unpublished doctoral dissertation, University of Wisconsin, Madison, WI.

Dale, H. (1994a). Collaborative research on collaborative writing. *English Journal, 84*(1), 66–70.

Dale, H. (1994b). Collaborative writing interactions in one ninth-grade classroom. *Journal of Educational Research, 87*(6), 334–344.

Dale, H. (1996). Dilemmas of fidelity: Qualitative research in the classroom. In G. Kirsch & P. Mortensen (Eds.), *Ethics and representation in qualitative studies of literacy* (pp. 77–94). Urbana, IL: National Council of Teachers of English.

Damon, W. (1984). Peer education: The untapped potential. *Journal of Applied Developmental Psychology, 5*, 331–343.

Deering, P.D., & Meloth, M.S. (1990, April). An analysis of the content and form of students' verbal interactions in cooperative groups. Paper presented at the annual meeting of the American Educational Research Association, Boston, MA.

Dembo, M., & McAuliffe, T. (1987). Effects of perceived ability and grade status on social interaction and influence in cooperative groups. *Journal of Educational Psychology, 79*, 415–423.

Dewey, J. (1938/1974). *Experience and education.* New York: Macmillan.

DiPardo, A., & Freedman, S.W. (1988). Peer-response groups in the writing classroom: Theoretic foundations and new directions. *Review of Educational Research, 58*(2), 119–149.

Durling, R., & Schick, C. (1976). Concept attainment by pairs and individuals as a function of vocalization. *Journal of Educational Psychology, 68*, 83–91.

Durst, R.K. (1987). Cognitive and linguistic demands of analytic writing. *Research in the Teaching of English, 1*(4), 347–375.

Ede, L., & Lunsford, A. (1983). Why write . . . together? *Rhetoric Review, 1*(2), 150–157.

Ede, L., & Lunsford, A. (1985). Research in collaborative writing. *Technical Communication, 32*(4), 69–70.

Ede, L., & Lunsford, A. (1986). Why write . . . together? A research update. *Rhetoric Review, 5*(1), 71–81.

Ede, L., & Lunsford, A. (1990). *Singular texts/plural authors.* Carbondale: Southern Illinois University Press.

Elbow, P., & Belanoff, P. (1989). *Sharing and responding.* New York: Random House.

Emig, J. (1971). *The composing processes of twelfth graders.* Urbana, IL: National Council of Teachers of English.

Ervin, E., & Fox, D.L. (1994). Collaboration as political action. *Journal of Advanced Composition, 14*(1), 53–71.

Faigley, L., Cherry, R.D., Jolliffe, D.A., & Skinner, A.M. (1985). Theories of composing. In L. Faigley, R.D. Cherry, D.A. Jolliffe, & A.M. Skinner (Eds.), *Assessing writers' knowledge and processes of composing* (pp. 3–22). Norwood, NJ: Ablex.

Faigley, L., & Miller, T. (1982). What we learn from writing on the job. *College English, 44,* 557–569.

Fleming, M.B. (1988). Getting out of the vacuum. In J. Golub (Ed.), *Focus on collaborative learning: Classroom practices in teaching English, 1988* (pp. 77–84). Urbana, IL: National Council of Teachers of English.

Flower, L. (1979). Writer-based prose: A cognitive basis for problems in writing. *College English, 41*(1), 19–37.

Flower, L. (1994). Teachers as theory builders. In L. Flower, D.L. Wallace, L. Norris, & R.E. Burnett (Eds.), *Making thinking visible: Writing, collaborative planning, and classroom inquiry* (pp. 22–33). Urbana, IL: National Council of Teachers of English.

Flower, L., Burnett, R.E., Hajduk, T., Wallace, D., Norris, L., Peck, W., & Spivey, N. (1990). *Making thinking visible: Classroom inquiry in collaborative planning.* (Project Book: Carnegie Mellon University.) Pittsburgh: Center for the Study of Writing.

Flower, L., & Hayes, J.R. (1980). The cognition of discovery: Defining a rhetorical problem. *College Composition and Communication, 31,* 21–32.

Flower, L., & Hayes, J.R. (1981a). A cognitive process theory of writing. *College Composition and Communication, 32*(4), 365–388.

Flower, L., & Hayes, J.R. (1981b). The pregnant pause: An inquiry into the nature of planning. *Research in the Teaching of English, 15*(3), 229–243.

Flower, L., & Higgins, L. (1991). *Collaboration and the construction of meaning.* Technical report no. 56. Berkeley, CA: Center for the Study of Writing.

Flower, L., Wallace, D.L., Norris, L., & Burnett, R.E. (1994). *Making thinking visible: Writing, collaborative planning, and classroom inquiry.* Urbana, IL: National Council of Teachers of English.

Forman, J., & Katsky, P. (1986). The group report: A problem in small-group or writing processes? *Journal of Business Communication, 23,* 23–35.

Freedman, S.W. (1987). *Peer response in two ninth-grade classrooms.* Technical report no. 12. Berkeley, CA: Center for the Study of Writing.

Freedman, S.W. (1992). Outside-in and inside-out: Peer-response groups in two ninth-grade classes. *Research in the Teaching of English, 26*(1), 71–107.

Freire, P. (1970). *Pedagogy of the oppressed.* (Trans. M.B. Ramos). New York: Continuum.

Gagne, R.M., & Smith, E.C. (1962). A study of the effects of verbalization on problem solving. *Journal of Experimental Psychology, 63*(1), 12–18.

Gardner, H. (1983). *Frames of mind.* New York: Basic Books.

Gere, A.R. (1990). Talking in writing groups. In S. Hynds & D. Rubin (Eds.), *Perspectives on talk and learning* (pp. 115–128). Urbana, IL: National Council of Teachers of English.

Goldstein, J.R., & Malone, E.L. (1985). Using journals to strengthen collaborative writing. *The Bulletin of the Association for Business Communication, 48*(3), 24–28.

Gong, G., & Dragga, S. (1995). *A writer's repertoire.* New York: Harper-Collins.

Heap, J.L. (1989). Collaborative practices during word processing in a first-grade classroom. In C. Emihovich (Ed.), *Locating learning: Ethno-graphic perspectives on classroom research* (pp. 263–288). Norwood, NJ: Ablex.

Higgins, L., Flower, L., & Petraglia, J. (1992). Planning text together: The role of critical reflection in student collaboration. *Written Communication, 9*(1), 48–84.

Hilgers, T. (1987). Young writers facing a new collaborative writing task. *Journal of Research in Childhood Education, 2*(2), 108–116.

Hill, C.E. (1990). *Writing from the margin: Power and pedagogy for teachers of composition.* New York: Oxford University Press.

Hillebrand, R.P. (1994). Control and cohesion: Collaborative learning and writing. *English Journal, 83*(1), 71–74.

Hillocks, G., Jr. (1986). *Research on written composition: New directions for teaching.* Urbana, IL: ERIC Clearinghouse on Reading and Communication Skills.

Humes, A. (1983). Research on the composing process. *Research in the Teaching of English, 53*(2), 201–216.

Johnson, D.W., & Johnson, R.T. (1979). Conflict in the classroom. *Review of Educational Research, 49*, 51–70.

Johnson, D.W., & Johnson, R.T. (1985). The internal dynamics of cooperative learning groups. In R. Slavin, S. Sharan, S. Kagan, R. Hertz-Lazarowitzc, C. Webb, & R. Schuck (Eds.), *Learning to cooperate, cooperating to learn* (pp. 103–124). New York: Plenum.

Johnson, D.W., & Johnson, R.T. (1994). Cooperative learning in the culturally diverse classroom. In De Villas, R.A., et al. (Eds.), *Cultural diversity in schools: From rhetoric to practice* (pp. 57–73). New York: State University of New York Press.

Johnson, D.W., Johnson, R.T., Roy, P., & Zaidman, B. (1985). Oral interaction in cooperative learning groups: Speaking, listening, and the nature of statements made by high-, medium-, and low-achieving students. *The Journal of Psychology, 119*(4), 303–321.

Kahn, E.A., Walter, C.C., & Johannessen, L.R. (1984). Making small groups work: Controversy is the key. *English Journal, 73*(2), 63–66.

Kirby, D., & Liner, T. (1988). *Inside out: Developmental strategies for teaching writing.* 2nd Ed. Portsmouth, NH: Boynton/Cook-Heinemann.

Kohn, A. (1986). *No contest: The case against competition.* Boston: Houghton-Mifflin.

Lakoff, R. (1973). Language and women's place. *Language and Society, 2,* 45–79.

Langer, J.A., & Applebee, A.N. (1987). *How writing shapes thinking: A study of teaching and learning.* Urbana, IL: National Council of Teachers of English.

Larson, C.E., & LaFasto, F.M.J. (1989). *Teamwork: What must go right, what can go wrong.* Newbury Park: Sage.

Locker, K.O. (1992). What makes a collaborative writing team successful? A case study of lawyers and social workers in a state agency. In J. Forman (Ed.), *New visions of collaborative writing* (pp. 37–62). Portsmouth, NH: Heinemann.

Lockheed, M. (1985). Sex and social influence: A meta-analysis guided by theory. In J. Berger & M. Zelditch, Jr. (Eds.), *Status, rewards, and influence* (pp. 406–427). San Francisco: Jossey-Bass.

Maimon, E. (1979). Talking to strangers. *College Composition and Communication, 30*(4), 365–369.

Matsuhashi, A., Gillam, A., Conley, R., & Moss, B. (1989). A theoretical framework for studying peer tutoring as response. In C.M. Anson (Ed.), *Writing and response: Theory, practice, and research* (pp. 293–316). Urbana, IL: National Council of Teachers of English.

Meeker, B., & Weitzel-O'Neill, P.A. (1985). Sex roles and interpersonal behavior in task-oriented groups. In J. Berger & M. Zelditch, Jr. (Eds.), *Status, rewards, and influence* (pp. 379–405). San Francisco: Jossey-Bass.

Miller, N., Brewer, M., & Edwards, K. (1985). Cooperative interactions in desegregated settings: A laboratory analogue. *Journal of Social Issues, 41,* 63–79.

Miller, N., & Harrington, H.J. (1990). A situational identity perspective on cultural diversity and teamwork in the classroom. In S. Sharan (Ed.), *Cooperative learning: Theory and research* (pp. 39–75). New York: Praeger.

Moffett, J. (1983). *Teaching the universe of discourse.* Boston: Houghton-Mifflin.

Morgan, M., Allen, N., Moore, T., Atkinson, D., & Snow, C. (1987). Collaborative writing in the classroom. *The Bulletin of the Association for Business Communication, 50,* 20–26.

Mugny, G., & Doise, W. (1978). Socio-cognitive conflict and structure of individual and collective performance. *European Journal of Social Psychology, 8,* 181–192.

Myers, D.G., & Lamm, H. (1976). The group polarization phenomenon. *Psychological Bulletin, 83,* 602–627.

Noddings, N. (1991). Stories in dialogue: Caring and interpersonal reasoning. In C. Witherall and N. Noddings (Eds.), *Stories lives tell: Narrative and dialogue in education* (pp. 157–170). New York: Teachers College Press.

Nystrand, M., & Gamoran, A. (1991). Instructional discourse, student engagement, and literature. *Research in the Teaching of English, 25*(3), 261–290.

Nystrand, M., & Gamoran, A. (1996, April). The effects of classroom discourse on writing development. Paper presented at the annual meeting of the American Educational Research Association, New York, NY.

Nystrand, M., Gamoran, A., & Heck, M.J. (1992). *Using small groups for response to and thinking about literature.* Center for the Organization and Restructuring of Schools. Madison, WI: Wisconsin Center for Educational Research.

O'Donnell, A.M., Dansereau, D.F., Rocklin, T., Lambiotte, J.G., Hythecker, V.I., & Larson, C.O. (1985). Cooperative writing: Direct effects and transfer. *Written Communication, 2*(3), 307–315.

Onore, C. (1989). The student, the teacher, and the text: Negotiating meanings through response and revision. In C.M. Anson (Ed.), *Writing and response: Theory, practice, and research* (pp. 231–260). Urbana, IL: National Council of Teachers of English.

Palincsar, A.S., Stevens, D.D., & Gavelek, J.F. (1989). Collaborating with teachers in the interest of student collaboration. *International Journal of Education, 13*(1), 41–53.

Parker, G.M. (1990). *Team players and teamwork.* San Francisco: Jossey-Bass.

Perl, S. (1979). The composing processes of unskilled college writers. *Research in the Teaching of English, 13*(4), 317–336.

Perret-Clermont, A.N. (1980). *Social interaction and cognitive development in children.* New York: Academic Press.

Peterson, P.L., Wilkinson, L.C., Spinelli, F., & Swing, S.R. (1984). Merging the process-product and the sociolinguistic paradigms: Research in small-group processes. In P.L. Peterson, L.C. Wilkinson, & M. Hallinan (Eds.), *The social context of instruction: Group organization and group process* (pp. 125–153). New York: Academic Press.

Phelps, L.W. (1989). Images of student writing: The deep structure of teacher response. In C.M. Anson (Ed.), *Writing and response: Theory, practice, and research* (pp. 37–67). Urbana, IL: National Council of Teachers of English.

Pianko, S. (1979). A description of the composing processes of college freshman writers. *Research in the Teaching of English, 13*(1), 5–22.

Rogers, P.S., & Horton, M.S. (1992). Exploring the value of face-to-face collaborative writing. In J. Forman (Ed.), *New visions of collaborative writing* (pp. 120–146). Portsmouth, NH: Heinemann.

Ross, J.A., & Raphael, D. (1990). Communication and problem-solving achievement in cooperative learning groups. *Journal of Curriculum Studies, 22,* 149–164.

Rubin, D.L. (1988). Introduction: Four dimensions of social construction in written communication. In B.A. Rafoth & D.L. Rubin (Eds.), *The social construction of written communication* (pp. 1–33). Norwood, NJ: Ablex.

Rubin, D.L., & Greene, K. (1992). Gender-typical style in written language. *Research in the Teaching of English, 26*(1), 7–40.

Sharan, S. (1980). Cooperative learning in small groups: Recent methods and effects on achievement, attitudes, and ethnic relations. *Review of Educational Research, 50*(2), 241–271.

Slavin, R.E. (1980). Cooperative Learning. *Review of Educational Research, 50,* 315–342.

Slavin, R.E. (1989). Research on cooperative learning: An international perspective. *Scandinavian Journal of Educational Research, 33*(4), 231–243.

Smagorinsky, P. (1991). *Expressions: Multiple intelligences in the English class.* Urbana, IL: National Council of Teachers of English.

Sommers, N. (1980). Revision strategies of student writers and experienced writers. *College Composition and Communication, 31*(4), 378–388.

Spear, K. (1993). *Peer-response groups in action.* Portsmouth, NH: Heinemann.

Sperling, M. (1990). I want to talk to each of you: Collaboration and the teacher-student writing conference. *Research and the Teaching of English, 24*(3), 279–321.

Sperling, M. (1993). *The social nature of written text: A research-based review and summary of conceptual issues in the teaching of writing.* (NCTE concept paper no. 8). Urbana, IL: National Council of Teachers of English.

Spurlin, J.E., Dansereau, D.F., Larson, C.O., & Brooks, L.W. (1984). Cooperative learning strategies in processing descriptive text: Effects of role and activity level of the learner. *Cognition and Instruction, 1*(4), 451–463.

Tammivaara, J.S. (1982). The effects of task structure on beliefs about competence and participation in small groups. *Sociology of Education, 55,* 212–222.

Tobin, L. (1991). Writing between the lines. In J.L. Collins (Ed.), *Teaching and learning language collaboratively* (pp. 63–71). Portsmouth, NH: Boynton/Cook-Heinemann.

Trimbur, J. (1985). Collaborative learning and teaching writing. In B.W. McClelland & T.R. Donovan (Eds.), *Perspectives in research and scholarship in composition* (pp. 87–109). New York: Modern Language Association of America.

Vail, N., & Papenfuss, J. (1989). *Daily oral language.* Evanston, IL: MacDougal, Littell.

Vygotsky, L.S. (1978). *Mind in society: The development of higher psychological processes.* Cambridge, MA: Harvard University Press.

Vygotsky, L.S. (1981). The genesis of higher mental functions. In J.V. Wertsch (Ed.), *The concept of activity in Soviet psychology* (pp. 279–299). Armonk, NY: Sharpe.

Vygotsky, L.S. (1931/1986). *Thought and language.* Cambridge, MA: MIT Press.

Wallace, D.L. (1994a). Supporting students' intentions for writing. In L. Flower, D.L. Wallace, L. Norris, & R.E. Burnett (Eds.), *Making thinking visible: Writing, collaborative planning, and classroom inquiry* (pp. 204–222). Urbana, IL: National Council of Teachers of English.

Wallace, D.L. (1994b). Teaching collaborative planning: Creating a social context for writing. In L. Flower, D.L. Wallace, L. Norris, & R.E. Burnett (Eds.), *Making thinking visible: Writing, collaborative planning, and classroom inquiry* (pp. 48–66). Urbana, IL: National Council of Teachers of English.

Warburton, T.L. (1987). The ABC's of group communication: A primer for effective group performance. *Journal of Technical Writing and Communication, 17*(3), 303–315.

Webb, N. (1982). Student interaction and learning in small groups. *Review of Educational Research, 52*(3), 421–445.

Weiner, H.S. (1986). Collaborative learning in the classroom: A guide to evaluation. *College English, 48*(1), 52–61.

Wittrock, M.C. (1974). Learning as a generative process. *Educational Psychologist, 11*, 87–95.

Author

Helen Dale is associate professor of English at the University of Wisconsin–Eau Claire, where she teaches courses in composition, literature, English education, and cultural diversity. A high school teacher for eleven years, she received her Ph.D. from the University of Wisconsin–Madison. She is the 1992 recipient of the American Educational Research Association's Steve Cahir Award for Research on Writing and was a finalist in the 1994 National Council of Teachers of English Promising Researcher Award competition. Her research interests include collaborative writing, supervision of student teaching, discourse analysis, and qualitative research. Among her publications are articles about co-authoring in the *Journal of Educational Research* and *English Journal,* and a chapter about the ethics of qualitative classroom research in *Ethics and Representation in Qualitative Studies of Literacy.*

This book was typeset in Palatino by Susan H. Huelsing.
Typefaces used on the cover were Eddmond, Spinoza, Futura, and Veljovic.
The book was printed on 60 lb. Finch Opaque by Braun-Brumfield, Inc.